THE

CARIBBEAN CONFEDERATION.

With a Map.

*A PLAN FOR THE UNION OF THE FIFTEEN
BRITISH WEST INDIAN COLONIES,*

PRECEDED BY

AN ACCOUNT OF THE PAST AND PRESENT CONDITION OF THE
EUROPEANS AND THE AFRICAN RACES INHABITING THEM,

WITH A

TRUE EXPLANATION OF THE HAYTIAN MYSTERY,

*In which is embodied a Refutation of the Chief Statements made by
Mr. Froude in his recent Work, "The English in the West Indies."*

BY

C. S. SALMON,

LATE PRESIDENT OF NEVIS;
FORMERLY COLONIAL SECRETARY AND ADMINISTRATOR OF THE GOVERNMENT
OF THE GOLD COAST;
CHIEF COMMISSIONER SEYCHELLES ISLANDS, ETC.;
MEMBER OF THE COMMITTEE OF THE COBDEN CLUB.

NEGRO UNIVERSITIES PRESS
NEW YORK

Originally published in 1888
by Cassell & Company, Ltd., London

Reprinted 1969 by
Negro Universities Press
A DIVISION OF GREENWOOD PUBLISHING CORP.
NEW YORK

SBN 8371-1833-6   74-6780

PRINTED IN UNITED STATES OF AMERICA

PREFACE.

THE West Indies are largely—indeed, chiefly—inhabited by
black people, whose ancestors were taken from Africa within
two centuries. These people are increasing in the West Indies,
and are certain to continue to do so. It is important, therefore, to study them seriously.

It is a fact beyond dispute that the African race is increasing everywhere where it has a foothold. It increases rapidly in
Brazil. It increases in the Southern United States. In the
mighty African continent where it has its home it has not
increased within the last two or three centuries due to religious
wars, invasions, and the slave wars and forays of export slavers;
but latterly, and since these have been somewhat mitigated in
ferocity and have become less frequent, the people are undoubtedly steadily increasing in their millions.

It is a fact, therefore, that the black contingent of the
human family, represented by the African, shows every probability of being, at all events as regards numbers, a great
force in the world of the future, in Africa and in America.

The civilisation of the African races is a question about
which a good deal has yet to be learnt. In Africa there are
places where the native races are living in rather well ordered
communities, and where the native governments show undoubted capacities for rule over wide regions. But there is
no recent record of a great State which we should call stable
or permanent being ever established ; that is to say, one lasting

through centuries. We know of numbers of relatively powerful States to have arisen, but they seem to have lacked cohesion, and to have been easily broken up by invasion from without or disruption from within. Religious wars have had much to do with this condition of things.

But we only know of these movements in comparatively recent times, and we only know them very partially. There are legends, universal among Africans, of powerful States of their people in the olden days, lasting for long periods. But there are no monuments extant to our knowledge, or written records, to guide us in these matters.

We are probably face to face here with a degeneracy from some superior social organisations that got broken up in the past.

The African as an individual is very remarkable, because almost anything can be made of him. We are, therefore, forced to admit that if circumstances ever arise which allow of any considerable body of Africans in their own country acquiring some of the arts and learning of modern times, they might found a powerful State of a permanent character. The people are brave ; with leaders of their own, and modern arms which are no respecters of persons, they might some day take it into their heads to claim their country for themselves.

The great thing against the African, and the real objection to him in the eyes of European races, is the fact that he is black, and, in most cases, his features are of the negro type, and he has wool instead of hair. Some black African races, however, have refined features with their wool. This question of colour, of features, and of wool, requires explanation, because it evidently has nothing to do with the mental capacity of the man ; they are, perhaps, consequences due more to climate than to anything else. But with Europeans the association of ideas leads all of them to deem this colour, these features, and this wool, to be signs of permanent inferiority.

There is nothing whatever to prove this beyond the belief

that the African has not yet developed a higher civilisation to our knowledge than we see him now possess. But this only throws him back behind ourselves scarcely a thousand years, and there may be circumstances to show why he is so far late. Do we deem ourselves any less than those who preceded us a thousand years ago?

We have all of us received helping hands. Had any European race been treated as the Africans have invariably been treated from time immemorial, it would have probably disappeared altogether. Had it survived it could certainly have never taken a place of honour or of value among the people of the earth.

The point aimed at in this book is to show the fitness of the black British subjects in the West Indies for admission into the communities of the British Empire, by allowing them, together with the white races in these colonies, to share in the privileges of British subjects everywhere—by having a full share in their local self-government. Where the machinery of local self-government does not now exist, in accordance with British ideas, it is urged that the same be at once set up. It is recommended to unite the whole British West Indies into one confederacy.

In Africa the people have forms of local self-government almost everywhere. They are forms of government in Africa which Europeans out there never or rarely study ; but by their working, as far as it has become known, the average competency of the people to manage them is undoubted. The formation and upholding of great and powerful States require other qualities, or, more correctly speaking, they require opportunities, which the African has not yet possessed.

It is impossible to dissociate the black British subjects in the West Indies from the kindred races of Africa ; what one may be the other may be. If the British people and their Government fail to place their black fellow-subjects in the West Indies on an equal footing within the Empire with the white races, they will be using their position to perpetuate a wrong, or rather to prolong it, for in all human probability to perpetuate it they will not be able. They will be prolonging a social and a political blunder. By giving the black subjects of the Crown some of those rights they themselves enjoy, the British people will be using for a good purpose that position of vantage they now possess ; a position which enables them to do that which will be an honour to themselves and a profit to the Empire.

Distinguished men like Mr. Froude recently, and Mr. Anthony Trollope many years ago, and other less noted names at intervals of time, have visited the West Indies more or less hurriedly, and their views of our black fellow-subjects have had wonderful currency amongst us. It can be fairly said that these views have been put forth without that adequate study of the subject—not necessarily on the spot—which its importance demands. A powerful writer, backed by a great intelligence, can write a pleasant book on very slight materials by the help of a trained intellect. ʳ The history of the African races has yet to be written. It is a pity that writers of the above stamp did not handle the subject more seriously, when it embodied the history and qualifications of one of the largest, and one of the growing, divisions of the human family.

CONTENTS.

1

THE

CARIBBEAN CONFEDERATION.

———•◇•———

CHAPTER I.

MR. FROUDE'S BOOK, "THE ENGLISH IN THE WEST INDIES."

MR. FROUDE always writes with an object. What then is the
purport of this book of his? It is not an account of the
British West Indies, for out of the fifteen colonies Mr. Froude
only visited four, and he landed but for a few hours at two
others. In the four that he visited he remained altogether
only a few weeks, and during those few weeks he lodged
chiefly with governors and officials, and spent his time in con-
verse with prominent people. And yet Mr. Froude deals with
the people—the blacks and the whites—the very few he saw
and the very many he did not see—and talks of them, and
confers on them certain characters, aims in life, capacities for
good and evil, and such-like, as if he had spoken with them all
and had known them all for a whole lifetime. Mr. Froude
speaks like one with authority, like a master sure of his
subject, the intricate details of which he had mastered and was
familiar with. Mr. Froude objects very much to modern
hasty methods; but the most self-asserting and meteoric of
newspaper correspondents would never venture on doing what
Mr. Froude has done.

Then what is the object of this book? The British black
man is depicted in it—very much of him—but none of his
acquaintances can recognise him. The Englishman in the
West Indies is there also; in this picture one can trace a

resemblance, but not an accurate likeness. Nature, as painted by Mr. Froude, is there in all its glory. When passing through a country on a coach, or even by express, one can realise the landscape ; and if one has the endowments and trained intellect of a Mr. Froude, one may try and paint it. But the men we pass on the roads, or see stationed on the hill-sides, or observe at work in their fields—what can we say of them ? We can talk of their physique and their appearance, picturesque or not picturesque, and no more.

Then what is the object of this book ? It is not written to give a true account of the British black man, for even Mr. Froude has to study a subject before he can teach us anything about it. The truth is, Mr. Froude has done that which has often been done before, but chiefly by Frenchmen. In the days of the Second Empire, French writers of eminence, who were not permitted to give their views on French matters politic, came over to England, and then returned to France and wrote a book about England. England was the text, but the preachers had other purposes in view and wandered very, very far off from it. By this ingenious method they were enabled to give their theories a body and shape, and make them pass under our gaze just as if they had been put into practice in real life. They were able to air their theories to their hearts' desire, and make them magnificent indeed. The pleased Briton saw himself depicted as the impersonation of every manly virtue and all political wisdom : this was when the writer wanted a model of this nature to drape with his theories. At other times the Briton saw himself made into something very mean indeed : this was when the writer wanted to dish up a warning to his fellow-countrymen. To these Frenchmen the Briton was a mere figure all along ; they never even tried to study him.

In England there is no censure on the press, and Mr. Froude need not have done as so many eminent Frenchmen did. He could have written all that he has said about the British black man in his cabinet at home. But we should have lost a great deal ; we should have lost those glowing pages about scenery and nature in the West Indies.

On the other hand, if Mr. Froude had not gone to the West Indies for his few weeks' trip, he could hardly have given us those theories of his under such an authoritative guise. He would have had to say what he really meant to say like the rest of us, according to facts, without making them appear to be the result of studies on the spot. The British black man in the West Indies is used by Mr. Froude as a figure only; he drapes him to suit his argument, just as the Frenchman did the Briton, and Mr. Froude has found the plan a good one. The theories of Mr. Froude may be good or they may be bad, but one thing is certain, the black figure he drapes for us nowise resembles the British black man as he lives in the West Indies.

What then is the object of this book? Its object is to put before us in a pleasant way Mr. Froude's theories on government generally. At home the subject of self-government had been thrashed threadbare, and it was impossible for even Mr. Froude to put life into it. So Mr. Froude went to the West Indies and returns with a figure of the British black man draped out of all recognition as a warning to Englishmen to avoid that unclean thing, local self-government. Mr. Froude stands behind the black man to deliver his blows at somebody nearer home. It is to be hoped the shield which covers this assault may not be made to suffer too much in the struggle.

CHAPTER II.

THERE are some races of men admittedly superior to others, but there are no rules beyond those of their own forging which have made them so. History also proves that inequality in the comparative prowess and strength of races and of nations may be due as much to the falling-away and deterioration of rivals as to any practical advances made by themselves. The standard of superiority accepted by the world of to-day consists of the possession of power, privileges, and wealth—however acquired. This is practical and prudent. Social order among men is thereby maintained, and family life and society are founded and kept together. But none of these things are gifts given direct by nature or by God. They are advantages acquired by men through their own labour sometimes, sometimes by force and by fraud. There are other treasures possessed by civilised men of more value than the above, if less prized; they are the languages, religions, arts, sciences, histories, and traditions of nations that have passed away. All these possessions constitute the inherited and transmitted gifts from men to one another. They also make up the whole of what a generation can leave to its successors. The children of the generations as they succeed one another may be thereby placed in a position which will enable them to make a better use of their faculties than some other men who are disinherited.

Men have an inheritance—that of their surroundings—always tainted with viciousness, prejudice, and ignorance. They live and act up to this, and it makes them what they are. Institutions gradually get formed for the purpose of transmitting to future ages this power and wealth, this security and public order. But experience having taught men how easy it is to lose a position which has taken much labour to acquire, they work later on to consolidate it, and to secure it against all possible risk of loss. It is the false direction of these efforts that so often leads to the eventual falling off. The fear of change and the narrow-minded dread of being ousted from a supremacy cause them eventually to hinder whatever may remotely lead to the loss of their relative position of superiority in the world. They no longer labour for their own advancement only ; they exhaust their best efforts to obstruct the advance of others. They are now working against the Providence of God ; their aims become more and more wholly material, and all the miseries of low desires grow apace in the state. Finally, the sickness of intellectual immobility brings on death,

> " For 'tis his nature to advance or die :
> He stands not still, but or decays, or grows
> Into a boundless blessing, which may vie
> With the immortal lights, in its eternity.''

The empire, with its institutions, its laws, its power and glory, and, at times, even the traces of the race that made it, are swept away and obliterated.

Nothing lasts but acquired superiority, kept abreast of the times by the untiring efforts of the successive generations. We know that types get renewed by descent, but of the body only. The mind can be so early influenced by its immediate surroundings that it also often gets credited with equal hereditary qualities to those of the body. But although we see ordinary intellectual types renewed in men, they are not so hereditarily. This is an everyday experience. The greatest intellects die out of the world never to be renewed in our times. We have had but one Shakspeare and one Burns. How mental types get renewed in the young intellects of the world we know not ; we observe only that the mind is influenced from the moment of its creation. We know that feeling conveys knowledge as well as sight does, and that the imponderable forces of the world are at their work around us always, but we cannot tell how. Man to be true to himself must be true to nature, and to do this he must act in accordance with the Divine Will. Let a man vigilantly do his best to assist nature, and the seeds of knowledge will be deposited where they will

germinate. The mental qualities that exist among men may
thus at each successive stage of development be propagated by
the touch of sympathy and the aid of practical study and
application. But the perpetual renewal by education in its
various forms is necessary, or the light will die out of the body.

Men are daily putting up images, hollow phantoms, and
idols of unreal worth, and tearing them down on finding them
false, while the genuine and substantial force that is hourly
brought into the world is wasted or not allowed to grow.
Hence arise two mighty evils : we lose the vital strength so
seriously needed ; and we feed a lesser growth that chokes our
development and keeps drawing us back into barbarism.
Every effort to keep a race of men to its lower type or in an
inferior stage of civilisation, nay, every acquiescence in such a
condition of things, is to work against nature and the Divine
Will. The shortsighted selfishness of men blinds them to this
folly and this crime. They assign to themselves perpetual
dominion as their due, to others slavery as their inheritance.
The fall is then not far off. If the curbed race accept
bondage as their lot, believing any endeavours on their part to
rise out of it to be useless, they will make no efforts. Their
masters and governors for an opposite reason—being entirely
contented with their position—will be satisfied to remain as
they are ; the natural rank accorded them, they feel, makes
them independent of any special efforts of their own. This
sentiment is a force of great power in the world everywhere,
but we can see it at work, and may study its effects, more
distinctly in the West Indies than almost anywhere else.

Little indeed have these islands to offer that can be of
interest to those not immediately dealing with them. The
utter lack of concern about their future among the British
public is entirely intelligible. How indeed can a people such
as the British—noble, generous and great—deem it worth their
while to aid, except languidly and against the grain, to keep up
a system which would perpetuate the degradation of a race for
the gratification of instincts and desires in which nothing can
be discerned but the love of gain ?

It is impossible to read the literature connected with the
British West Indies, that has been published during the past
fifty years, without a feeling of profound dejection. England
has been here for over two centuries in her might, and we read

of nothing to warrant us in saying she has done her duty. Everyone depicts the lowness to which human nature may fall; many tell us that the degradation is without remedy; some even say we should profit by it for pecuniary ends. Mr. Froude regrets the old slavery days. Some amongst us may regret that days still more distant cannot come back, or rather the men that lived in them. The Christianity of the time of St. Augustin was familiar enough with slavery, but the great Christian masters did not deem the slaves inferior to their owners in those natural and moral qualities which they knew the Creator placed at the disposal of all mankind. St. Augustin, in his North African bishopric, must have been familiar enough with black races, and he tells us : "human nature is one." In his "City of God" he tells us how material progress is nothing, if it has to be paid for at the cost of moral progress. With what terrible words he would overwhelm the apologists who would maintain that we did our duty in relegating the African to a lower order of civilisation, sometimes even to a different order of creation, than our own.

> " God created man in his own image ;
> In the image of God created he him."

No one is born with knowledge. In each individual it has to be acquired through the faculties given him. It is these faculties that make the man, and not the diverse uses to which he puts them. How he uses his faculties or whether he uses them at all are different questions. This view does not lessen the value of any man's self-acquired qualities and of learning ; it only puts them in their place. They are earned abilities of which all men are equally, but diversely, susceptible, and therefore they vary. The powers and intelligence the Creator has given to man are the all-potent instruments everyone of us possesses. It is the good uses to which a man puts these instruments during his lifetime on earth that constitute superiority. It is the non-usage of these instruments that constitutes inferiority.

CHAPTER III.

THE AFRICAN AS HE IS IN AFRICA.

MR. FROUDE has visited Southern Africa as well as the West Indies. His opinion of the British black man in the latter place is dealt with in another chapter. His views about the African in Africa are dealt with in this chapter. This is what Mr. Froude says, pages 124, 125, 126 :—

" Before my stay at Barbados ended, I had an opportunity of meeting at dinner a negro of pure blood who has risen to eminence by his own talent and character. He has held the office of Attorney-General. He is now Chief Justice of the island. Exceptions are supposed proverbially to prove nothing, or to prove the opposite of what they appear to prove. When a particular phenomenon occurs rarely, the probabilities are strong against the recurrence of it. Having heard the craniological and other objections to the supposed identity of the negro and white races, I came to the opinion long ago in Africa, and I have seen no reason to change it, that whether they are of one race or not, there is no original or congenital difference of capacity between them, any more than there is between a black horse and a black dog, and a white horse and a white dog. With the same chances and with the same treatment, I believe that distinguished men would be produced equally from both races, and Mr. ——'s well-earned success is an additional evidence of it. But it does not follow that what can be done eventually can be done immediately, and the gulf which divides the colour is no arbitrary prejudice, but has been opened by the centuries of training and discipline which have given us the start in the race. We set it down to slavery. It would be far truer to set it down to freedom. The African blacks have been free for thousands, perhaps for tens of thousands of years, and it has been the absence of restraint which has prevented them from becoming civilised. Generation has followed generation, and the children are as like their father as the successive generations of apes. The whites, it is likely enough, succeeded one another with the same similarity for a long series of ages. It is now supposed that the human race has been upon the planet for a hundred thousand years at least, and the first traces of civilisation cannot be thrown back at farthest beyond six thousand. During all these ages mankind went on treading in the same steps, century after century, making no more advance than the birds and beasts. In Egypt or in India or one knows not where, accident or natural development quickened into life our moral and intellectual faculties ; and these faculties have grown into what we now experience, not in the freedom in which the modern takes delight, but under the sharp rule of the strong over the weak, or the wise over the unwise. Our own Anglo-Norman race has become capable of self-government only after a thousand years of civil and spiritual authority. European government, European instruction, continued steadily until his rational tendencies are superseded by a higher instinct, may shorten the probation period of the negro. Individual blacks of exceptional quality, like Frederick Douglas in America, or the Chief Justice of Barbados, will avail themselves of opportunities to rise, and the freest opportunities ought to be offered them. But it is as certain as any future event can be that if we give the negroes as a body the political power which we claim for ourselves, they will use it to their own injury. They will slide back into their old condition, and the chance will be gone of lifting them to the level of which we have no right to say they are incapable of rising."

"Chief Justice R—— owes his elevation to his English environment and his English legal training. He would not pretend that he could have made himself what he is in Hayti or in Dahomey. Let English authority die away, and the average black nature, such as it now is, be left to assert itself, and there will be no more negroes like him in Barbados or anywhere."

Chief Justice R—— of Barbados is doubtless a British black man. His ancestors, for aught we know, may have been African chiefs ; had his parent not been made a slave of by Englishmen the son would not have graced the British bench, but there is nothing to show he would not have been the Prime Minister of some African potentate, or a man of weight in his own country.

It is impossible altogether to separate in Mr. Froude's book his opinion of the African in Africa from his opinion of the British black man in our West Indies : for the purposes of his argument he combines the opinions he has drawn from both sources, and the man served up to us represents in reality neither the African in Africa nor the West Indian African. But the above as well as the following extract will sufficiently show Mr. Froude's general opinion of the Africans in Africa, his conclusions as to the value of the assistance they have received from Europeans, and the importance of its being continued. In pages 286, 287, he says :—

"One does not grudge the black man his prosperity, his freedom, his opportunities of advancing himself ; one would wish to see him as free and prosperous as the fates and his own exertions can make him, with more and more means of raising himself to the white man's level. But left to himself, and without the white man to lead him, he can never reach it, and if we are not to lose the islands altogether, or if they are not to remain with us to discredit our capacity to rule them, it is left to us only to take the same course which we have taken in the East Indies with such magnificent success, and to govern blacks and whites alike on the Indian system.   The circumstances are precisely analogous.   We have a population to deal with, the enormous majority of whom are of an inferior race.   Inferior I am obliged to call them, because as yet, and as a body, they have shown no capacity to rise above the condition of their ancestors except under European laws, European education, and European authority to keep them from making war on one another."

Does Mr. Froude, could any man, seriously contend that the efforts of Europeans, English or other, in any West Indian Island, or anywhere in Africa, have been other than such as must inevitably tend to a further degradation of the race they enslaved or held dominion over? To argue otherwise is the mere perversion of history.

But let history speak for itself.   No more in Africa than in the West Indies will it require any commentary.   The African races have one great fact against them : there is no record of their ever having done anything to shape the world's history. This is a reproach now often brought to the front to show their incapacity.   Mr. Froude uses it, and men of lesser eminence employ it, to show how completely they are unfitted to be self-governing and the masters of their own destiny.   This alleged want of self-governing power in the black races of Africa as we know them to-day is by no means self-evident, and we are groping very much in the dark indeed when we go any distance back.   Bacon says that time, like a river, only floats down to us the things of light weight, while the solid treasures remain for ever buried in its depths.   But from the African races we have received nothing, at least nothing that we know of.   The ancient civilisations of Northern Africa may have been beholden to them for something ; but if so, we have no record of it.   But all this of itself is no proof whatever in support of Mr. Froude's contention that the African people are unfitted for self-government.

The somewhat stationary condition of the black races of Africa is due to their not having yet written on stone or in books.   Victor Hugo, in his " Notre Dame de Paris," paints with a force never equalled the effects of architecture on the character and civilisation of a people ; it is the creator of all the arts and sciences ; it gradually calls them

all to its aid, until, strong themselves, they can stand alone.
We see a polished state arise whose powerful civilisation had
its origin in a rude temple of unhewn stone.   The ephemeral
buildings of the Africans are as writings on sand, they never
last the lifetime of a generation. The son has to begin where
the father begun, and ages upon ages pass away without a
yard's advance.   The only things that remain over from the
times long ago are the superstitions and vague traditions
handed along, as we see the like handed along among every
race and people on the globe.

In justice we must also consider the force of tropical
vegetation. There are people now in the world, the stranded
remnants of mighty nations, whose poorness of spirit and backward condition would never betray their origin, were it not
for the mighty records left by their remote ancestors, and
which time has not yet altogether effaced.   There may never
have been such records in tropical Africa, but, if such exist,
they are buried perhaps for ever in the densities of jungle and
forest.

Then the next greatest teacher as regards time, but not
as regards results, is also unknown to the African ; he has
never written in books. The knowledge that can be wrung
from nature and from man himself, in a single generation,
is slight indeed. Without writing of some kind this knowledge
is ephemeral ; it gets lost. The savage man knows nature only
as an animal.   Let him be able to record his experiences,
and in ten generations this accumulated knowledge will bring
the dawn of a civilisation.

A greater evil for the African than all the others combined
is that he owes nothing to any other people.   For centuries
his coasts have been ravaged by every civilised nation in the
globe, not one of whom has given him aught but chains.
Every civilised people owe most of their culture to foreigners,
and to records that yet subsist of nations that have passed
away. Why have the Central Africans learned nothing ?   They
had the greatest civilisations of the ancient world on their
borders.   But this is just where we are in profound darkness ;
perhaps in the olden times there was something here.   Enough
for us to know now that for ages and generations the whole
of that belt of Africa north of the Equator, stretching from
ocean to ocean, has been swept and ravaged by successive

invaders. They passed as the waves of the ocean pass, wiping out every record. Even to this day the ravage continues, and from the trembling lips of fugitives may be heard the fearful tales of towns overturned, whole tribes annihilated or passed into slavery, and cultivated provinces made into deserts. These are the Mohammedan invasions from the north, and slave-hunting and other inroads from the east.

Until quite recently the African blacks have been regarded as the helots of the human race, and Mr. Froude would have us revive and perpetuate the tradition. England herself was among the first to set up on the African coast the barracoon of the export slaver. Then wars redoubled, then ferocity was added to ferocity, and cruelty to cruelty. The avarice for gold and unscrupulous cupidity were added to the old horrors. For three centuries all Europe went on thus, all around the African coast, encouraging war and rapine—tribe against tribe, village against village—and we filled our coffers to repletion by the sweat and blood of Africa. Then came the revulsion, followed by the great act of justice in emancipation and suppression of export slavery. We now set up trumpery governments and dummy protectorates, and very real lines of custom houses all along the coast to receive the black man's tribute—and we introduce the gin-bottle.

And yet Africans live and multiply, and if Europeans would only let them alone entirely there would be 300 millions of them in course of time ready to buy our cottons, our hardware, and our machinery, and we should make more money than ever we did before out of them. Of civilisation nothing need be said, for even had any already existed, the concerted action of Europe must have stamped it out long ago. Only the deepest self-sufficiency of a conceited hypocrisy, added to the profoundest ignorance of the subject, could have expected any civilisation worth the name to have been introduced by Europe, or to have lived.

A civilised state possesses the capital accumulated by different races of men through successive generations of labour. This capital is laid out and employed by the citizens under the guidance of their inclinations, and they reap the harvest that merit or opportunity puts in their way. The accumulations will be both those of industry and of the intellect, and the greater or less power put into action in the using of these represents the more or less vitality of the people.

But a people without this capital may labour as hard as men can, and yet they will never get beyond a hand-to-mouth existence, varied by famines. This is the Africa of to-day. Much of the backwardness may be due to the faults of her own people, but assuredly her chief misfortunes and misery are due to enemies and deadly influences she was too divided, or not strong enough, to contend against. Some people seem to believe that all Africans are about the same in appearance and in character, and that the atrocities of Dahomey and Ashanti are repeated all over the continent. But the truth is that Africa is a world in itself, and contains within its limits more diversities of people, with greater differences in their institutions, habits, and beliefs, than any other quarter of the globe. The military aristocracy of Ashanti was a power of quite recent growth, and among those who know something of its inner workings, and the objects held in view by the chief councillors of the people, not all are of opinion that its practical destruction by England has been a gain to Africa—the terrible executions notwithstanding. As a power it was despotic, cruel, and ruthless. But almost from its inception it came into contact on the coast, at only 120 miles from its capital, with the Portuguese, the Dutch, the English, and other European nationalities, who offered to buy all the men, women, and children they could get. The legitimate expansion of Ashanti was also hindered by England, from the beginning of her protectorate policy on this part of the African coast, for petty local reasons. Had the Ashantis been left alone, had we made allies of them as we might well have done, in exchange for the abandonment of their bloody customs, had they known Europeans only as legitimate traders, the chances are there would have been now at this part of Africa a native power, a real native power, open to legitimate influences, and the nucleus of an important native civilisation.

It is a great mistake to assume that there are no useful political organisations in Africa. We hear most about the military despotisms of Ashanti and Dahomey, and the executions kept up for the chief purpose of inspiring dread in the ruled. But there are countless provinces the European public never hear of, or hear of but faintly, composed of confederated tribes whose chiefs meet regularly in council, where order and peace are maintained ; the hegemony being usually in some walled village where a chief of ancient descent lives a patriarchal life respected by his people.

If the truth must be told, England has done perhaps more than any other nation to. retard the advance of the Africans in Africa. She has established nothing whatever ; she has retarded a good deal. On two or three spots she has collected a few thousand Africans together and got some of them to adopt the outward varnish of a spurious European civilisation. But she never allows a native power, or a native chief, to possess or gather together any national strength within range of her influence, her protectorates, or her dominions. It is possible Africans may never develop a civilisation which will be an exact counterpart to that of Europe. England's efforts, so far, have been in the direction of denationalising the people rather than in the more hopeful one of encouraging their self-development. If a church is built, the congregation is expected to appear in black coats and hats as if Christianity and civilisation itself were inextricably allied to the present conventionalities of Europeans. England has failed utterly everywhere, and after three hundred years of dominion on the coast as slave-hunters, warriors, traders, and missionaries, she finds herself, as regards any influence for good, very nearly in the same position as at starting. Where Frenchmen introduce the Roman Catholic religion, it is with the afterthought of inclining the people to be politically well-disposed towards France ; Englishmen introduced Protestantism as much with the view of getting the natives to incline to the side of England as for the purpose of civilising them. It is only recently that independent religious bodies and congregations have been formed with which black ministers of African nationality are associated, and these bodies have done and are doing the work which should have been commenced three centuries ago.

Those who know something of Africa and its numerous races admire the sterling common sense and practical ability of those Africans who have been reached by the right methods, and feel quite certain in their own minds that the people of this mighty continent, if only they get fair play, are as capable of making a fit use of a high-class civilisation as any other people are, and that they are as competent to govern themselves at this moment as the average of mankind. This is all proved by facts on the spot. It is easy to pick but on the African continent examples enough to bear testimony for almost any theory—for or against the African race—so great is the diversity. But there is one thing of which there can be no doubt whatever in any candid mind, and that is that European dominion has been often a curse and has never been of any service to the African people. We find Kroomen, Yoloffs, and others make the most excellent sailors; we find several tribes equal to the Jews and Parsees for their trading and money-making qualities; we meet men everywhere who are easily transformed into excellent mechanics; we find the majority of the people brave and resolute in war; Stanley and Livingstone had men to stand by them after a manner unsurpassed in the pages of history for fidelity, endurance, foresight, and pluck; if rightly approached we find the people capable of religious fervency and steadfastness; if supplied with schools we see them eagerly filled; if scholarship be put in their way we see them acquire it and retain it, and, what is more and better, we see them become masters in their turn to pass on the torch to their backward brethren. They love the Bible, and become expert theologians, fitted to found sees and to gather together and direct congregations. As evangelisers and missionaries, the blacks among their own people in Africa have done more real good in ten years than all the Europeans in three centuries. These are facts. Of the civil policy of the majority of the nations, peoples, and tribes, among themselves, we know relatively nothing. When we say they are unfitted for this, that, and the other thing, we are merely conjecturing to ourselves when we are not talking nonsense. In Africa it is not an uncommon circumstance to come across a people whose chief ruler is never allowed to see the sea. Wondering, we consider this a mark of the most senseless barbarism. But it is in reality a sign of extreme wisdom and profound policy. The sea and its coasts were made the dread of Africa. The coast to this day is the most backward and uncivilised part of the whole continent. The civilisation of the slave-dealer and the gin-bottle has left its mark. In reality the people of Africa must be possessed of great natural parts to have made so much of that which was presented to them; they garnered every grain of good seed that came in their way ; they were not always so successful in rejecting the bad.

Every civilised country in the world has owed its chief advancement and enlightenment to the sea ; the coast towns were ever the most policied ; from them spread inwards arts, sciences, religion, trade, civilisation in fine.   In Africa how different was all this !   For centuries the polished nations of Europe made its coasts everywhere a hotbed for vice, a centre of crime, a point from which was spread abroad devastation and rapine ; and now we sit down in our cabinets and point out how a people who have so little profited by the teachings of the outer world must be unfitted to rank among self-governing communities.

CHAPTER IV.

THE armed feats of England by sea and land in the waters of the Caribbean Sea and the islands that gem its bosom are justly deemed by Mr. Froude amongst the most glorious in her annals, and they will stand imperishable in the pages of the world's history.

But history might well have afforded to pass over in silence all else that the English have done in the West Indies, because they have done little to deserve being remembered. Even the magnificent pages of Mr. Froude cannot mend this. But he has now brought "the English in the West Indies," as colonists and governors, before the bar of the public opinion of the world, and the verdict will be that, in the past, they have grievously misused their privileges and much neglected their duties. Coupled with this verdict will be a severe condemnation of the Home Government which could have allowed, if it did not connive at, such a deplorable state of things.

No eloquence can make the unlovely beautiful, or transform that which the natural instincts of our natures deem of little merit into useful deeds.

Men are given to actions bred of cupidity and selfish desires, even when their surroundings are ennobling and bracing, and they know it. It is because he sees this that a man of instructed intelligence seeks to place before himself and his household examples that breathe the purer atmosphere of religion, poetry, romance, and the records of worthy deeds. He hopes thus that his children will be better than he is himself. Sometimes by contrast and as a warning he holds up the mirror which shows the reverse side of human nature, so that the lesson may be inscribed on the young intelligence that meritorious actions

only can bring good. The history of the inner life of the
British West Indies may be used for the latter purpose, but
scarcely a single line of it will serve as an example to be
followed.

When the people of the United Kingdom were paying
three times the price they now pay for sugar, the estates in the
West Indies were in a " flourishing " condition. A number of
English landowners were reaping large incomes, and merchants
and managers were making fortunes. The British black man
also was contented, for slavery had recently been abolished,
and he could always get food and the little shelter he needed if
he chose to work for them. In the island of Trinidad and
in some other localities he could do more; he could earn the
wherewithal to indulge in drink, debauchery, and vice. Some
of the most instructively warning pages of West Indian history
deal with these debased instincts of the recently manumitted
British slave, and the peculiar remedies suggested by the planters
and their government to overcome the evil.

But to this material prosperity there were other drawbacks
besides the evil habits of the poor uninstructed slave. For
while a purely animal existence was nearly all that was deemed
necessary for the people, or that was meted out to them, the
rich whites were thought to have fulfilled all the duties they
owed to themselves and to society by indulging in an elaborate
and lavish hospitality. There was no movement among the
well-to-do and upper classes to establish anything whatever for
the education of the people or for the advancement of the
moral standard of the settlements from which they drew their
wealth.

What a contrast we see here at once between the West
Indian colonies of England and those other colonies of free
men where no servile class was known ! The history of these
latter colonies shows an unparalleled material progress, but this is
equalled, if not surpassed, by the efforts of their citizens to
reach the highest standards of mental and moral excellence.
With what delight will future generations read of noble institutions and efforts, and of equally noble results that will
assuredly follow !

But to return to a lesser standard of human existence. We
shall seek in vain among communities of freemen for a parallel
to anything to be met with in the history of the British West

Indies. No places in the world have made so many people of wealth as these islands. Wealth was largely made when it would have been difficult to fail in making it, and countless lesser fortunes were made under less favourable conditions. But this prosperity had no basis of strength. It came and was dissipated, and the chief traces of it to be met with to-day are parks and demesnes half obliterated by jungle. After the ruin of the old proprietary, whose ostentatious mode of life helped their downfall, the cultivation of exportable produce was carried on by absentee capitalists. This new condition of things rather intensified, if anything, the previous position.

But, nevertheless, a change was gradually coming over these islands. The white men were getting to be fewer. This was a distinct loss, for, although their predecessors had left undone those things they ought to have done, the best hope of the islands lay with them.

It was impossible for any advance to be made under slavery. After emancipation it has been equally impossible, due to the mismanagement of Governments. The whites of the pre-emancipation days, and those who immediately succeeded them, failed in doing anything for these islands, but this was due to their vicious surroundings, and to their position as slave owners, not to any other causes. After all they were English-men, but Englishmen in a false position, with the best instincts of their race neutralised for good.

On the downfall of direct slavery the local self-government which the whites had so far enjoyed came to an end. Downing Street then became the Providence of these islands. The position was not without its difficulties, but there were great opportunities for good. No good was done, perhaps none could have been done. The irresponsible bureaucratic system set up by Downing Street has been a failure from the beginning.

A savage believes if a man can be great for evil, he can be great for good in an equal degree. In a somewhat modified form the belief continues amongst us to this day, but the Government is the impersonation, and upon its altar we burn the incense. It is difficult to get people to believe that their prosperity depends but little on statutes and governmental interference. Governments have so much interfered, and have done so much harm and injustice that way, that people are apt to think they can do good in a like degree if they were only to try. This is a grave error; Governments can obstruct progress just as any opposing force in nature may do so, but human prosperity has always depended on the exertions of individual men and those local associated bodies whose actions they can control and direct. In a complicated form of society the general or imperial Government has its undoubted uses, but among these can never be reckoned those duties which men must perform for themselves as individuals or when associated together. These associated bodies have different names in different countries and under different conditions and circumstances, but, for all practical purposes, they are now classed under the one designation : "Local self-government." Buckle's statement, that the greatest service a government can do is to repeal the obstructive statutes of their predecessors, indicates the true functions of a general government.

Crown Government rule has been unaccountably praised by people whose judgment should have weight. Further inquiries make it usually appear that these eulogists had no experience of the circumstances of the people ruled, and had none of that particular knowledge which it is essential to possess before any opinion on such a matter should be given. The eulogists, however, evidently had much knowledge of the personal views and reports of the rulers.

The Colonial Office has been remarkable on the whole for the body of useful men it has had the good fortune to get to accept positions of trust in the West Indies. Perhaps this is the explanation why the reports of the various royal and official commissions that have been from time to time sent to the islands to inform Parliament of the work done by these gentlemen, as well as the accounts of the majority of distinguished travellers, have been so laudatory of the system of direct Crown Government. The reports and accounts have evidently been framed under the natural bias and impression that the rule of such a highly-trained and excellent body of men must be estimable anywhere.

We are accustomed in England to hear of Royal Commissions and their Reports, and sometimes, when the Commissions are strong ones, people refer to their Reports for authoritative guidance. But the Reports of the Royal Commissioners on Jamaica, four of the Windward Islands, and the Leeward

Islands, published in 1884, were received at the time, by those who had a knowledge of the questions dealt with in them, with surprise. The Reports were not even in accordance with the evidence attached to them ; in any case, they were incorrect, in discord with daily facts, and misleading. This was observed at the time by the public press, and the verdict then pronounced against these Reports cannot be too much insisted on. But these Reports, although so misleading, have, in the eyes of some people, an authority attached to them, due to the mere fact of their being termed Reports of Royal Commissioners. The two gentlemen who reported had evidently not studied the matters they dealt with in a manner sufficiently searching to warrant them in drawing the conclusions they drew. The Reports were planters' reports, written for the planters, and received by them with applause. By the bulk of the people of the colonies these Reports were received with some natural indignation ; and by the friends of the people, and of the colonies they live in, as integral parts of the British Empire, they were read with sorrow.

To show how incorrect they were, it will be only necessary to give paragraph 67, page 17, of "Report, Part IV., Supplementary Remarks " :—

" 67. In regard to the West Indian colonies in general, and to those in particular to which our Commission referred, we think it well to point out that, situated as they are within the tropics, among their inhabitants there can never exist anything approaching to a preponderating number of Europeans ; at the same time, their great fertility and power to export tropical produce will steadily attract to them English capital and enterprise, and considerable numbers of English residents will always be found in them for the purpose of administering and managing industrial undertakings. For instance, the considerable annual excess in the values of exports over imports is a sure indication that the produce exported belongs, together with the ensuing profits, to those resident elsewhere. But as the employers and employed will be, generally speaking, of different races, the Imperial Government will continue to have an ultimate responsibility in the administration of these islands, and must consequently retain an adequate proportion of direct power in the administration."

This extract shows at once the gist of the whole. The Reports were fitted to meet the circumstances of dependencies that it was evidently expected, or perhaps hoped, would continue to be composed of absentee landholders and a resident population of African and East Indian serfs. But although

four years only have elapsed since these Reports were published, they are already shown to be hopelessly impossible of ful-
filment. Peasant cultivators are multiplying so fast that everyone now admits that the land and the produce, in all the West
Indian Islands, will in the future be very largely the property of
the people residing in these islands, and cultivating for their
own profit. So that, after all, we shall have real colonies here,
and not that class of servile dependency that has hitherto been
so dishonourable to the British character and name, and which
is ever a weakness to an empire.

The Commissioners, by the above extract, in fact and in
substance, prophesied that these islands would always continue
to be servile dependencies, and would never be real colonies.
But if Cuba and Porto Rico contain over one million whites,
why cannot our British colonies contain resident white owners?
That they can do so is clearly shown in this and other chapters. If in the olden days there were five to ten times the
number of whites that are now resident in these British isles,
why should there not be the same or twice that number in the
better and larger future ?

The statement that the exports were so much in excess of
imports was formerly true, but it is getting to be less true, as
the following figures will show :—

In the six years ending 1871, the total exports from the
British West Indies were valued at 45 millions sterling, of
which the United Kingdom received 31¼ millions. The total
imports were 38 millions, of which the United Kingdom sent
17½ millions. During this period the total exports exceeded
the total imports by 7 millions sterling ; but the exports to
the United Kingdom exceeded the imports therefrom by
11¾ millions sterling.

In the six years ending 1877, the total exports were
49½ millions sterling, of which the United Kingdom received
34¼ millions. The total imports were 45 millions, of which
the United Kingdom sent 20½ millions. During this period
the total exports exceeded the total imports by 4¼ millions
sterling ; but the exports to the United Kingdom exceeded the
imports therefrom by 14 millions.

In the six years ending 1883, the total exports were
55½ millions, of which the United Kingdom received 34¼ millions. The total imports were 51¼ millions, of which 21 millions

came from the United Kingdom. During this period the total exports exceeded the total imports by $4\frac{1}{4}$ millions sterling ; but the exports into the United Kingdom exceeded the imports therefrom by $13\frac{1}{4}$ millions. In 1886 the total exports, £7,806,169, were only about 4 per cent. less than the total imports, £7,314,492.

The West Indies, therefore, have been lessening the balance against them, and the argument of the Royal Commissioners, founded on this condition of things, falls through. Those absentee landowners—including companies—who grow sugar and other produce have to pay for growing it, the same as resident owners, and if they are not permitted to make monopoly laws which would be unjust to resident labour and resident enterprise, the imports will have to balance the exports. The real unjust advantage these absentees enjoy is that they pay no taxes. They pay no taxes on the lands from which they raise £3,000,000 to £5,000,000 worth of produce annually. The Commissioners did not profess to be free traders ; indeed, their main recommendations run counter to this national system. It is satisfactory, therefore, to see them, as it were, in spite of themselves, laying down a free trade principle. Fair traders should take note of the argument ; they very forcibly state that an excess of exports over imports shows that the people residing outside the exporting country reap all the profits of this excess ; consequently an excess of imports over exports is a measure of the profit reaped by the people residing in a country.

But although the views of the Commissioners themselves on so many points are not to be reconciled with facts, the evidence they collected and attached to the Reports is of some value, if read with the necessary discrimination required in such cases.

The opinions of the local whites on the form of government they are under are easy enough to get at ; they cry them from the house tops. But the usual official interpretations of these opinions—which Mr. Froude also follows—are unjust and unworthy of those who give them. Mr. Froude, speaking of Trinidad, page 85, says :—

" Trinidad, as I said, is at present a Crown colony, the executive council and the legislature being equally nominated by the authorities. The popular orators, the newspaper writers, and some of the leading merchants in Port of Spain had discovered, as I said, that they were living under what they called 'a degrading tyranny.' They had no grievances, or none that they alleged, beyond the general one that they had no control over the finance. They very naturally desired that the lucrative government appointments for which the colony paid should be distributed amongst themselves."

In page 67 he says :—

"But it had pleased the Home Government to set up the beginning of a constitution again in Jamaica, no one knew why, but so it was, and Trinidad did not choose to be behindhand. The official appointments were valuable, and had been hitherto given away by the Crown. The local popularities very naturally wished to have them for themselves. This was the reality in the thing so far as there was a reality."

So that the time-honoured desire of Englishmen to have, in this case with their black fellow-subjects, some voice in the raising and spending of taxation—which has grown double in recent years—is interpreted, when out of England, to mean something very un-English indeed. The chapter on taxation will show that the Trinidad Englishmen had just cause to demand local self-government for the island.

Mr. Froude is not consistent in giving the views of West Indian Englishmen. In page 163 he says :—

"If the Antilles are ever to thrive, each of them also should have some trained and skilful man at its head, unembarrassed by local elected assemblies. The whites have become so weak that they would welcome the abolition of such assemblies."

But the whites of all the Antilles have precisely similar views to those of Trinidad, and they take care the same shall be known. It is easy for Mr. Froude to make the above statement ; he never visited any of the islands he evidently refers to except Dominica. As regards Dominica the statement is doubly misleading, because the whites of that island are notoriously known to have exactly opposite views to those Mr. Froude gives them. The Colonial Office has tried over and over again to get them to do as Nevis, St. Kitts, and Montserrat did, and commit the happy dispatch by aiding the Government in abrogating their assembly. The Colonial Office by lavish promises of great things to be done, and other methods known to administrators, in a weak moment got the people of the islands of St. Kitts, Nevis, and Montserrat to aid in abolishing their elective assemblies and in substituting the present dummies nominated by the Crown and outvoted by the officials. Ever since then the whites of these Antilles have bitterly regretted what they did. They have associations in every important centre, hold enthusiastic meetings, belabour the Colonial Office with petitions, and do everything that men fully persuaded in their own minds may do, by peaceful and constitutional methods, to get back their old assemblies, but with enlarged powers and a freer representation for all classes.

No one will accuse Mr. Froude of wilful misrepresentation, but he must have strangely shut his eyes to obvious facts, or the gentlemen around him must have gravely misled him, to cause him to be so blind. Whatever be the causes, such statements do infinite mischief, and they will cause doubts to be cast over the accuracy of those other parts of Mr. Froude's book which are of value.

The English in the West Indies of the present day are a very different body of men from the old slave-owners and planters whose disappearance Mr. Froude so regrets. Many among them are, as near as can be, a counterpart of colonists such as one may meet with in Canada or Australia—upright, shrewd, active men who know they must work for themselves and are not afraid to do so. Among the old families men are to be met of another type, men after Mr. Froude's frame of mind, who regret the past, who have no influence over the present, and who are destined to have none over the future. Mr. Froude doubtless saw all this, and he partly tells us so. He places but a meagre confidence in the whites of this and the coming generation of West Indians; he trusts them doubtingly. He therefore would subject them as well as the blacks to the iron rule of the Indian system.

Mr. Froude, however, tells us that a good deal of the ill-success of the British Government in the West Indies has been due to the Colonial Office not having selected the right men as governors. In page 91 he says :—

" Among the public servants of Great Britain there are persons always to be found fit and willing for posts of honour and difficulty if a sincere effort be made to find them. Alas! in times past we have sent persons to rule our Baratrarias to whom Sancho Panza was a sage—troublesome members of parliament, younger brothers of powerful families, impecunious peers ; favourites, with backstairs influence, for whom a provision was to be found ; colonial clerks, bred in the office, who had been obsequious and useful."

He says again in the page following :—

"The West Indies have been sufferers from another cause. In the absence of other use for them they have been made to serve at places where governors try their 'prentice hand and learn their business before promotion to more important situations."

As might have been expected, Mr. Froude has a word to say in favour of Governor Eyre, and he drops a tear over his fate. In page 260 he says:—

"But all that can be said against Mr. Eyre (so far as regarded the general suppression of the insurgents) is that he acted as nine hundred and ninety-nine men out of a thousand would have acted in his place, and more ought not to be expected of average colonial governors."

England thought differently, and the public opinion of the world thought differently, and they think differently now. But Mr. Froude is perhaps right in saying that the average colonial governor would have acted as Governor Eyre did, and would do so now under similar circumstances—if he dared, because men holding power under irresponsible bureaucratic systems always act thus—if they dare.

For all evils Mr. Froude has the one remedy : "Govern them as we do India." But what is the difference between the Indian system and this Crown Government rule he so much decries? The difference between tweedle-dum and tweedle-dee. Mr. Froude's objection to the present system consists chiefly in that in one or two islands a council exists, half the members of whom are elected by a restricted suffrage and the other half nominated by the Crown. Indeed, the majority of these legislative councils have half their body nominated by the Crown, the other half being made up of officials ! To complete the picture, these councils are one and all under the thumb of the governor and his officials, who, in their turn, are under the absolute guidance of Downing Street. What Mr. Froude really wants is "one man" rule. The direct rule of the strong man with a "free hand," as Warren Hastings had in India, with no troublesome questions as to his doings being asked or given. In page 174 he says :—

"Am I asked what should be done ? I have answered already. Among the silent thousands whose quiet work keeps the empire alive, find a Rajah Brooke if you can, or a Mr. Smith of Scilly. If none of these are attainable, even a Sancho Panza would do.   Send him out with no more instructions than the knight of La Mancha gave Sancho—to fear God and to do his duty."

No amount of extracts from Mr. Froude's work would exactly convey his meaning; his book in this respect resembles those wonderful West Indian dishes he speaks of, " with subtle differences of flavour for which no language provides names." His book is not only a long and terrible indictment against the black races of the world, but every page impresses one with the contempt in which he holds every institution and every system that has not for its sole object and aim the undivided sway of Englishmen over every race and people they happen to be among.   Nay, fearful that the dreaded form of liberty may appear amidst a people with whose interests some of the interests of the British Empire itself are bound up, but who do not happen to be of the Anglo-Norman race, he will prohibit Englishmen living among these people having any political influence, because he feels they will be compelled to share it with their fellow-subjects.

But Mr. Froude is not consistent even here.   Tyranny has ever been noted for capriciousness, and its advocates cannot escape the influences of the medium amidst which they or their imaginations dwell.   Speaking of Barbados, page 103, he says :—

" The Governor of Barbados is not despotic.   He controls the administration, but there is a constitution as old as the Stuarts ; an assembly of thirty-three members, nine of whom the Crown nominates, the rest are elected.   The friction is not so violent as when the number of the nominated and elected members is equal."

Here we see the working of a real constitutional system —for Barbados, differing from every other West Indian island, is almost an entirely self-governing colony—and the result is the most English, the most enlightened, the most advanced, and, on the whole, the most prosperous of the British West Indies.   It is not difficult to vituperate liberty in every other West Indian island, for none of its influences ever passed over any one of them.   Unalloyed personal rule has been their lot ever ; liberty need not defend itself from Mr. Froude's attacks here ; it could never have done any harm where it never existed.   But Mr. Froude

cannot see even this old Barbadian constitution, dating from
the Stuarts, and which has helped to make Barbados rise so
conspicuously above its neighbours, without giving it a kick ;
he says : " The system may have worked tolerably without
producing any violent mischief." But Mr. Froude must also
be inaccurate ; he continues : " There have been recent
modifications, however, pointing in the same direction as those
which have been made in Jamaica. By an ordinance from
home the suffrage has been widely extended, obviously as a
step to larger intended changes." In the direction of Jamaica !
But the suffrage and constitution of Barbados have always
been more liberal than in Jamaica, and the " ordinances from
home " have all to be passed by the local assemblies before
being approved of by the Secretary of State. The " widely
extended suffrage " of Barbados dates from before the recent
Jamaican constitution, and was in advance of it in every way.
There are 4,200 electors in a population of 180,000 in Barbados to 9,298 electors to a population of 620,000 in Jamaica.
This Barbadian suffrage would only alarm a Mr. Froude. In
a town a man must have a £5 a year freehold or be assessed
at £15 for parish rates or pay £2 a year taxes, and outside a
town he must pay £1 a year taxes. No menial may have a
vote, but anyone else who has a salary equal to £50 a year
may have one. Lodgers who pay £15 a year rent who live
on premises worth £50 pound a year may vote. Professional
men also have a vote, and all those holding degrees. And
Mr. Froude's Englishman of the West Indies trembles at this !

But it is not true now. The " English in the West Indies "
of the present day have learnt much, and the ruins scattered
so freely around them are witnesses enough that the past
systems were failures, and that a new and better system must
be brought in.

But it never was true. The " English in the West Indies "
never looked with favour on the absence of political rights.
In a book published forty-six years ago (in 1842), and written
by a distinguished and leading gentleman of Trinidad in those
days, the Honourable Wm. Hardin Burnley, Chairman of the
Agricultural and Immigration Society of the Island, designated
" Observations on the Present Condition of the Island of
Trinidad," &c., in Appendix F, occurs the following pregnant
sentence, which not only entirely disposes of Mr. Froude's

assertions, but practically accounts for much of the present low condition of all the islands :—

" Much of the policy of our Colonial Government will be found to be erroneous, and indeed positively repugnant to the growth and prosperity of our dependencies. The radical error of our system lies in conferring official appointments in the colonies, chiefly upon natives of Great Britain, and more particularly in making these offices exclusively dependent upon ministerial patronage. If this latter power were limited solely to the appointment of governors, leaving all other offices to be filled up in the colonies by the usual influences which bring men into place and power in England, it would be all that a just and necessary supremacy in the mother country would require. There would be no difficulty in finding competent persons to fill these offices, for the tendency of such a rule would be to attract talent in the colony instead of driving it out, as is the case at present ; for no man of wealth and independent feeling will submit to remain in a country where they find themselves and children virtually excluded from official rank, emolument, and political influence. They generally retire as early as they can to Great Britain, where they find themselves on an equal footing with others, and thereby denude the colony of floating capital and intelligence, which keeps it in a state of torpid inanimation."

The intelligent writer shows how in Canada the acute judgment of Lord Durham led him to detect this as the cause which made property more valuable on the American side of the border; for in, those days Canada was not endowed with local self-government. He also points out how it was the absence of a free self-governing power adjoining the British West Indies, with whose territories a comparison could be made, that caused the obviousness of the bad policy followed to be less apparent. But now we have territories adjoining the West Indies which are free and self-governing enough in all conscience, and, despite many drawbacks which should not be found in any British colony whatsoever, they are forging ahead and beating the West Indian colonies. Europeans are flocking to these places in thousands. Capital is pouring in, railways are being constructed, and the signs of activity and enterprise are abundant. Yet no one can say, and Mr. Froude most certainly would not, that either Yucatan, or Guatemala, or Salvador, or Costa Rica, or any other state of Central America, is politically a very stable government, or is inhabited by homogeneous races.

Let Mr. Froude's advice be followed, and the remaining whites in the British West Indies whose circumstances will admit of it will sell off and retire to Central America or to England, or to the United States or to some of the free colonies, and no fresh white colonists will ever settle in them.

In page 221 Mr. Froude says :—

"The pale complaining beings of whom I saw too many, seemed as if they could not be of the same race as the men who ruled in the days of the slave trade. The question to be asked in every colony is, What sort of men is it rearing? If that cannot be answered satisfactorily, the rest is not worth caring for."

In pages 284-5 he says :—

"The English of those islands are melting away. This is a fact to which it is idle to shut our eyes. Families who have been for generations on the soil are selling their estates everywhere and are going off. Lands once under high cultivation are lapsing into jungle. Professional men of ability and ambition carry their talents to countries where they are more sure of reward. Every year the census renews its warning. The rate may vary ; sometimes for a year or two there may seem to be a pause in the movement, but it begins again, and it is always in the same direction. The white is relatively disappearing, the black is growing ; this is the fact with which we have to deal."

Mr. Froude here confirms word for word the prophecy made by Mr. Burnley forty-six years ago, as before quoted. Of course Mr. Froude assigns an exactly opposite reason for this exodus to that of Mr. Burnley. But Mr. Burnley was a West Indian gentleman, and a recognised spokesman for the European community of his time ; and the exodus had then commenced for the forcible reasons he assigns. The reasons Mr. Froude assigns never existed. Nine-tenths of the resident whites in the West Indies at this day keep continually petitioning the Colonial Office for the form of local self-government laid down by Mr. Burnley. And what does Mr. Froude ask for on their behalf? In page 287 he says : "Govern them as we govern India . . . the blacks will be perfectly happy. . . . To the whites it would be the opening of a new era of hope." A new era of hope! Mr. Froude poses as the spokesman for the "English in the West Indies ;" but he sometimes has his doubts about their acceptance of his panacea ; for he again says in page 287 : "Should they " (the whites) "be rash enough to murmur" (at the above offer) "they may then be justly left to the consequences of their own folly." Every indication from the West Indies shows that the resident whites almost unanimously demand an extension of local self-government. Mr. Froude has not interpreted their sentiments.

Franklin says : " He that tells you, you can succeed in any way but by labour and economy, is a quack." This saying could be learnt with advantage in the West Indies as elsewhere. There are yet men, but a minority only, in these colonies who hope to succeed not so much by their own efforts as by the labour and economy of others. They know well enough what are the requisites for success, only they think they are entitled to the success while others are created to do the work and economy parts. Mr. Froude will cause some of them to persist in this belief, notwithstanding the discouraging signs that it no longer works as it did once. But even then it worked in a form of society Franklin had not in view. We can all understand a settlement where there were only planters and their slaves; where political economy, competition, wages of labour, and all such matters had no footing. This was the old condition Mr. Froude evidently so much admires, and whose disappearance he regrets, in our West Indies. We have now a new condition, but it is not yet a settled one. We have halted on the road, not able to retrace one step, but afraid to move forward. This condition is not conducive to local prosperity. Mr. Froude admits this much, but he tells us we must move backwards again, not to direct slavery no doubt, at least not so in name, but to a kind of serfdom ; a condition of things making the blacks permanent dependants of a rather well-to-do body of middle-class white planters. It is true this body of planters does not at present exist, but Mr. Froude thinks the East Indian administrative system, if applied to our West Indian colonies, would bring about the happy consummation. Mr. Froude may think so, and some very few others with him, but there is no analogy between the East and West Indies to argue on. No two places could be more wide apart. Everything is here that makes for difference. An argument on this basis must resolve itself into mere personal opinions. The East Indian form of government may be as admirable in its place as Mr. Froude deems it to be. But it is very un-English, and it is wholly unsuited to a colony or to the West Indies, just as the present system of irresponsible

bureaucratic rule is unsuited.   No body of whites of English,
or of any other, nationality would consent to settle and make
their homes in a country so ruled.   The Europeans in the
East Indies are a mere drop in that great ocean of humanity,
and if one may judge from their expressed sentiments, not one
of them ever went there to enjoy the " admirable " rule.

Let us be honest.   If Englishmen really wish to settle in
the West Indies, what is it that hinders them from going there ?
Some fear the climate.   Then the statements we so often hear
about the nature and character of the inhabitants must deter
many from making their homes among them.   There is no greater
enemy of these British possessions than he who spreads abroad
statements which bring into unpleasant prominence the vices
and weaknesses of the blacks.   This, however, would right
itself in time, for the good qualities of these people would also
leak out eventually, and fairly-minded men would strike a
balance, and find out that, after all had been said for and
against them, they were no worse than average humanity.
But the blacks are saddled with evil qualities and vices
they never possessed.   Among the detractors of the great
African section of the human family Mr. Froude can head
the list.   With good-natured contempt he allows them those
qualities which cannot be disassociated from a powerful and
even splendid physique, but he will scarcely allow they are
themselves entitled to use these qualities.   He allows them
nothing else.   If the West Indian whites are satisfied with
Mr. Froude's general estimate of them, no one else has any
right to complain.   He has painted them in their homes with
a master-hand.   We see them vividly before us with their
regrets, their hopes, their aims.   We see what they have been;
we see what they would wish to be.   We see the West
Indies of the old days; we see what Mr. Froude's whites would
like them to be in the future.   If all these pictures can
attract a single colonist from Great Britain, it will not be the
vigorous, the enterprising, or the manly.   But if man be un-
attractive, nature is great.   The physical splendour of these
islands and the teeming wealth of their soil, so eloquently set
forth for us by Mr. Froude, may overcome some natural
repugnance to the people which the perusal of his work
cannot fail to engender.   The ruin of the resident English
families in the West Indies is often referred to by Mr. Froude,

but he evidently has no knowledge of the chief causes of this ruin. Those he assigns are inadequate altogether. If a fall in the price of a produce or a cereal could permanently ruin landlords, the race would have become extinct long ago all over the world. They suffer losses—maybe severe losses—at times, and during depressions, and some may become bankrupt. But this no more kills them off as a body in a state than merchants, manufacturers, and traders get killed off by losses and bad times. They suffer as other people do, and no more.

But there were subtle causes at work in the West Indies which more surely sapped the prosperity of the whites than anything Mr. Froude has brought forward. Barbados was exempted from the infliction, and we see the result to-day in its favour. The Encumbered Estates Court Act for the West Indies was passed in 1854, and it was left optional with the islands to avail themselves of its provisions or not. The intention of the Act being to obtain a cheap and ready method for disposing of encumbered estates, most of the then local governments accepted it.

Now for the result. It is almost incredible, but nevertheless true. The action of the court from the commencement was opposed to the spirit and intention of its promoters. This is how it was worked. An owner of a property valued at say £10,000 gets someone to advance him money, say £2,000, to put up buildings and machinery, or otherwise work it more profitably, and he gives a regular mortgage on the property as security. Such a proceeding would not be uncommon anywhere. The English merchant in England who buys and sells the produce raised on this property, also supplies the owner and the estate with its various requirements. In course of time, by bad management of the owner, the estate comes to be indebted to the merchant, say for £5,000 or £6,000. This merchant is aware from the beginning that there is a mortgage prior to his claims on the properties for moneys advanced. This merchant, nevertheless, can carry his claim before the Encumbered Estates Court sitting in London and demand that the property be sold. The sale takes place, and there are few to bid. The estate realises about £6,000. Perhaps the merchant himself buys it. The court pays the merchant the whole of his claim, and the original mortgagee gets nothing. This is called the method of the "consignee's lien."

Some years ago when the writer was working for the abolition of this court, he was in communication with several gentlemen, among whom the late Sir T. Graham Briggs was the most eminent. In a letter dated the 8th January, 1882, Sir Graham says :—

"The existence of the Encumbered Estates Court and the precedence which they have given to the 'consignee's lien' or 'merchant's open account' over mortgage, settlement, or any other claim without reference to date—or in reference to justice—the inevitable result of which must be to throw eventually all the land in the islands into the hands of the merchant, that is, of absentee proprietors. . . . I cannot imagine anyone, not a trading merchant, deliberately putting capital into any colony where this law existed. . . . I think that no island can continue to thrive where this law, so fatal to capital and energy, has existed for many years. No one, not a merchant trading with that particular island, dare advance the smallest sum on mortgage even if the property be perfectly free and unencumbered ; no man can be sure of any settlement on his wife or children, although he may die not owing a penny. It is impossible that men with small capital, who are the backbone of every community, can purchase land unless they pay down the whole of the purchase money."

On the 11th April, 1882, he writes :—

"The question of the abolition of the Encumbered Estates Court is of the most vital import to everyone who has property in the West Indies, and above all to the wives and children of such, for at present they are liable to be shamefully robbed under the Encumbered Estates Court without any chance of safety or of redress."

In his evidence before the Royal Commissioners at Nevis Island in 1883, Sir Graham Briggs said : "The inevitable tendency of this rule (of the consignee's lien) is, of course, to wipe out the resident proprietors."

In their Report on the Leeward Islands the commissioners themselves state that the working of the Encumbered Estates Court was one of the causes of the backward condition and loss of population in those islands.

Speaking of Jamaica they said : "Industrial progress and prosperity are very seriously checked at the present time by the shyness of capitalists to invest their capital in Jamaica. A main cause of this is the fact that no security can be obtained for advances by means of mortgages on real property."

For thirty years and more this court operated in these unfortunate islands, driving away capital and enterprise, except such as the close corporation of British West Indian Merchants chose to advance. These merchants, having thus the game in their hands, had the proprietors at their mercy. These latter were obliged to ship all their produce to their consignees, even if better prices were ruling in the West Indian ports than in London. They had to use the ships of the consignees on these latter's own terms. They had to accept the prices the consignees sold for. They had to grow the produce the consignees preferred to deal in. The consignees discouraged the growth of every produce but sugar.

This court was abolished only eighteen months ago. But no business man can doubt that such a phenomenally stupid, disastrous, and iniquitous law, after being in operation for so many years, must have left its mark, and destroyed thousands of the homes of the old English settlers.

It is thus Mr. Froude misleads; he sees an effect, but he assigns the wrong causes. It suits his theory to give the wrong causes; if it had not he would have gone beneath the surface of things to find the true causes.

There have been other causes at work in the West Indies besides those already mentioned, which have tended to drive away white settlers, but which Mr. Froude, naturally, does not refer to either. Indeed, had he referred to these causes, and given them their proper weight, some of the most remarkable chapters in his book would have remained unwritten.

At the close of the seventeenth century the cultivation of sugar-cane was introduced into the West Indies. The cultivation of this product has always paid best when carried out on large estates and by gangs of labourers living in camps. This is much due to the fact that the growth of cane and its subsequent manipulation sometimes require about one adult per acre. An 800 acre estate, in full cultivation, will want 600 adults at least, in some West Indian islands—a very different condition of things to that with which we are familiar in England. Before the general adoption of this cane cultivation, the resident whites were numerous in the British West Indies, as numerous in proportion to the blacks as in the Spanish colonies. Mr. Froude says differently, but he is wrong. In Nelson's time the little Island of Nevis alone, where the great admiral was married and resided for a time, had thousands of white inhabitants, and a very effective local self-government.

Mr. Froude fails to give the correct reasons for the white population not disappearing from the Spanish West Indies as they did from the English. They did not disappear because the cultivation and trade of the Spanish islands did not wholly turn to sugar. Tobacco, coffee, and many other products of a like class continued to be grown in sufficient quantities, and the local trade and circumstances of these larger islands gave employment to many Europeans; and the people were not handed over to a merchant monopoly.

After the adoption of sugar-cane cultivation throughout the British islands there came a change. Europeans with a small acreage and small means could not make a sugar estate pay so well as those who had larger estates and greater means. Gradually the smaller estates got absorbed in the larger. This put a stop to immigration of Europeans. The class from which they are usually taken found no profitable field for their operations in these islands, now becoming more and more the property of a few resident, and a large number of absentee, sugar estate owners. The work of the islands was henceforth carried on by slaves and their hired supervisors.

Before the introduction of sugar-cane the land was profitably cultivated by resident owners of small properties, who raised coffee, spices, fruits, cotton, and other arboreous cultivations. This kind of cultivation can be carried on more profitably on a small acreage, under the direct supervision and active control of the owner, than on large estates. The advent of the sugar-cane, and the great profits it brought to capitalists and large land-owners, killed the middle-class emigrant, by ousting the only industry by which he could live.

Another change is again coming over these islands. The sugar-cane has ceased to pay in those places where it cannot be cultivated cheaply. It is now open to the same competition as corn, and, like corn, it must give way to those other forms of cultivation which are better suited to the localities. Hence, in all the West Indies, we see a gradual return to the old system of cultivation which prevailed during the seventeenth century. Mr. Froude sees this change, and evidently regrets it, but he has failed to grasp, or to give us, the true causes. It is not therefore wonderful that he should go astray about the remedies. His remedy is the one thing for all maladies: "Rule these colonies as we rule India," and the white man will come back again.

We now see the West Indies passing into the hands of small proprietors; this is inevitable. But the Englishman is not among them; this is open to be remedied. Of course there are difficulties. In the olden times we had the West Indies only. Now we have colonies at least as attractive. The emigrant is a man eminently given to follow his own inclinations, and he is as little likely to go to the West Indies as they are to-day as he would be to go to the West Indies Mr. Froude would make for him.

If England transforms her West Indies into one great colony whose people—white and black—have a voice in the management of their own concerns, they will come before the world, emerging from the dark clouds that now envelop them, and attract English colonists. The great landowners and others interested financially in these colonies will also have to make up their minds. There are large estates in the islands going to waste, and others only partially cultivated. The holders hold on hoping for some movement that will bring back the sugar-cane to the old prices. That day will never come. Why not form syndicates in England to parcel-up and sell these properties outright to the thousands of young Englishmen who will buy them and go out and work on them? The Englishmen will go, as they went before, on condition they have a future for themselves and their families after them. They do not fear the blacks, and they need not fear them. But Mr. Froude has done much mischief here. The blacks will work well, but only on condition they get good wages. Let a man be prepared to pay good wages and treat his labourers as he would treat English labourers, and he will be certain to succeed in the West Indies.

CHAPTER V.

THE AFRICANS IN THE WEST INDIES—

THE BRITISH BLACK MEN.

THE Africans in the West Indies, or the British black men, are very different beings, as will be presently shown, to the creatures depicted by Mr. Froude.

Mr. Froude's object in giving us such an incorrect and misleading picture of the black races in our West Indian Islands has been already suggested in the first chapter.

Before Mr. Froude, or any other man, could feel himself justified in making such sweeping and wholesale statements about a people, he should at least make sure of his ground by a study of the subject. The British West Indies consist of fifteen colonies; two are on the mainland, the others being islands or groups of islands. It has been seen that Mr. Froude only visited four islands out of all this, and, of these four, one was Jamaica, an island 144 miles long with a superficies of over 4,000 square miles. The population is about 620,000, of whom less than 15,000 are whites. Mr. Froude saw the people of one town and its environs. He landed at the Island of Trinidad—at Port of Spain—and made several small expeditions into the settled neighbourhood. He landed at the Island of Dominica and saw even less of the people than he did at either of the before-mentioned two islands. He landed at Barbados, but here he saw more of the people, the island being smaller and flatter, and the chief of the police drove him across it with a fast trotter. He stopped in each island about fourteen days—in the neighbourhood of the town he landed at. It is necessary to insist on these points. In a book of ordinary travels one does not care whether a writer stopped an hour or a year at a locality; we read for pleasure or amusement, not for instruction. But Mr. Froude would not only amuse and delight, he wishes also to instruct us. We are all glad to be instructed by Mr. Froude, but we must stipulate that he shall master his subject before discoursing so dogmatically on it.

What should we think of a Frenchman who went to Wales, landed at Cardiff, spent a fortnight with his consul, made a few calls in the neighbourhood, and had a few walks and drives about the environs, and then returned to France and wrote an account of the Welsh people he never saw, and about whom he could know nothing except by hearsay? Such things have been done, no doubt, but then no one pays any attention to what such people say.

·Mr. Froude is exactly in this position, only that Englishmen pay a great deal of attention indeed to what he has to say. He is distinguished as an historian and a brilliant writer; everyone admits this, and Englishmen are proud of him. But this makes the responsibility for exactitude the greater. No man, however eminent he may be, is entitled to mislead.

In these days great writers have even wider influence than orators, and they employ the same machinery of public print to obtain hearers. Mr. Froude is one of Britain's most renowned discoursers, and every word he sends abroad on the wings of the press is read and spoken of wherever Britons congregate. In a splendidly written passage, page 36, he says :—

"Oratory is the spendthrift sister of the arts, which decks itself like a strumpet with the tags and ornaments which it steals from real superiority. The object of it is not truth, but anything which it can make appear truth; anything which it can persuade people to believe by calling in their passions to obscure their intelligence."

What is the moral difference between spoken and written words? It depends on the faculties of a man which method he uses to convince us. In theology sometimes the preacher, sometimes the writer, wields the most influence. One man is a trained speaker, the other is a trained writer. Both have the like object in view—to further a cause they have at heart. Both often pursue the same methods in argument. But if there be some excuse for an orator who, in the heat of action, amidst the ringing cheers of admirers, oversteps the limits of truth, there is not the same excuse for a writer who does this thing in his cabinet.   But here we have Mr. Froude condemning the British black man without having sufficiently seen or studied him.   It is doubtful if the opinions he gives us are even at second-hand—taken from the few whites of his own way of thinking who naturally flocked round him at the islands.   All his opinions on the matter would seem to have been the result of prejudices formed in England long ago, if we may judge from what he has to say of a negro boy who was a fellow-passenger on the steamer that took Mr. Froude to the West Indies :—

"There was a small black boy among us, evidently of pure blood, for his hair was wool and his colour black as ink.   His parents must have been well-to-do, for the boy had been in Europe to be educated.   The officers on board and some of the ladies played with him as they would play with a monkey.   He had little more sense than a monkey, perhaps less, and the gestures of him grinning behind gratings and pushing out his long thin arms between the bars were curiously suggestive of the original from whom we are told now that all of us came."

Poor black boy ! poor son of a despised race !   He was young and inexperienced, and did not sufficiently measure the distance that separated him from the superior beings who made sport of him.

After his visit to the four islands this is Mr. Froude's opinion of the British black man.

In page 49 he is describing some black men he saw on board an intercolonial steamer :—

"Evidently they belonged to a race far inferior to the Zulus and Caffres, whom I had known in South Africa.   They were more coarsely formed in limb and feature.   They would have been slaves in their own country if they had not been brought to ours, and at the worst had lost nothing by the change."

Slaves were brought to the British West Indies from every region of Western Africa.   To rightly study the question raised here by Mr. Froude, a knowledge of Africa itself is necessary ; a knowledge not of South Africa but of that part of Africa where the slaves usually came from.   We must see the people in their homes before we can tell offhand, like Mr. Froude can, that they were improved, or made no worse, by being carried off into bondage.   Among all the Africans we carried into slavery those about and behind Lagos were incontestably the most ill-looking physically. Sorrowful to relate, the Akus *are* ugly. As a matter of fact, however, they are also among the most intelligent peoples of all Africa. As traders they are beating the English out of the African rivers ; as missionaries they equal the best sent from Europe ; as industrious cultivators of the soil they are not surpassed by the French peasant ; they are seen among the councillors of the governments in Western Africa, and are reckoned the most intelligent. They are barristers ; they are doctors. They are as ubiquitous in Western Africa, where money is to be made, as Scotsmen are in England. They live in large, well-laid-out mud-walled towns, and have defeated the Dahomeans in many a well-contested field, fighting for home and freedom. But they often lost prisoners in battle—ill-looking, ugly men, no doubt, but valiant ; these the Portuguese bought and re-sold to us when we did not buy them ourselves direct. It would appear the descendants of these people have not improved in physique or appearance under British bondage. At least we have Mr. Froude's testimony to this effect.

Speaking again of the British black man, Mr. Froude says, page 49 :—

"Morals in the technical sense they have none, but they cannot be said to sin, because they have no knowledge of a law, and therefore they can commit no breach of the law. They are naked and not ashamed. They are *married* as they call it, but not *parsoned*. The woman prefers a looser tie that she may be able to leave a man if he treats her unkindly. Yet they are not licentious. I never saw an immodest look in one of their faces, and never heard of any venal profligacy. The system is strange, but it answers. . . . There is evil, but there is not the demoralising effect of evil. They sin, but they sin only as animals, without shame, because there is no sense of doing wrong. They eat the forbidden fruit, but it brings with it no knowledge of the difference between good and evil. . . . In fact these poor children of darkness have escaped the consequences of the Fall, and must have come of another stock after all."

The above is Mr. Froude's opinion of the British black man as he is to-day, after being over two centuries under the direct rule of England. Sir Spencer St. John's Haytian is a highly-civilised man in comparison. But other Englishmen have been in the West Indies besides Mr. Froude, and they are Englishmen who have a right to speak about the people, because they know them. The following are taken from statements by Sir Anthony Musgrave, late Governor of Jamaica, who had an intimate acquaintance extending over years with all the West Indies. In a letter to the *Times*, under date September, 1883, he says :—

> "The true present condition and character of the negro labouring population is also much misunderstood ; and, in treating of it, sufficient allowance is not made for the condition fifty years ago, of which the present state of things—so far as it is objectionable—is the outgrowth. Much stress is laid upon the terrible figures of illegitimacy ; but few pause to remember that little more than fifty years ago it was not permitted to teach the fathers and mothers of these people to read ; they were prevented, or at least discouraged, from marriage, and were encouraged to breed like cattle. Now, we turn up our eyes in shocked amazement at their awful depravity. Have we much excuse for surprise that the lessons then inculcated are not yet unlearnt ? "

The Report of the Royal Commissioners on the Leeward Islands said, when referring to illegitimate births : "The traditions on the subject remaining over from the days of slavery are still strong enough to deter many negroes from regarding marriage as a necessity."

Oh history ! how you can be mangled to suit the views of partisans ! What Mr. Froude would make us believe to be a defect in the moral fibre of the African race, is shown to be the direct consequences of our own base conduct and vile and unclean teaching in the past. Can an Englishman read this and not blush for his nation, were it true? "*The system is strange, but it answers*" ! A foreigner reading Mr. Froude might well deem it *did* answer, and that we kept the people in this loathsome condition from policy. Verily, if the African has escaped the consequences of the Fall, he has not escaped the consequences of West Indian rule.

Nor has he ; besides the above well-authenticated reasons given by Governor Musgrave, there are others that have arisen since emancipation, and which have put obstacles in the way of marriage. These are the excessively low wages usually given, but for which the Government is not responsible, and the enormous duties on food, which make living so expensive and the keeping up of a decent household difficult for the poor, and for this the Government is responsible. But these points will be separately dealt with in the chapters on taxation and labour. We know in England that good wages and prosperous times increase the marriage rate. The same causes operate in the West Indies that operate everywhere else.

But although the harm done by slavery was great, and has left vestiges unhappily not yet altogether obliterated, Mr. Froude, for reasons best known to himself, has grossly exaggerated the position. This misstatement of his is of a serious nature, and is perhaps the most misleading in his book. Such unions as they were permitted to make in the days of slavery were ever deemed binding by the people. Those who broke them were their masters and mistresses, when purposes of gain made it expedient for them to separate and break up the family of the poor slave. Even those unions that are not now consecrated by marriage are usually deemed binding. All that remains to be said on this subject will be found in the chapter " Religion in the West Indies."

The returns of the Registrar-Generals' departments in the several West Indian colonies show the number of legal marriages among the black population, in proportion to births and deaths, to be not greatly different from similar proportions among European nations. When Mr. Froude says the black people are not venally licentious, he is right, just as it would be right to say the same of the English people, but if he means more he is wrong. There are erring men and women among the West Indian blacks as there are amongst English men and women, certainly no less, probably no more.

Further on. page 106, Mr. Froude says :—

" The personal influence of the white man over the black, which might have been brought about by a friendly intercourse after slavery was abolished, was never so much as attempted. The higher class of gentry found the colony more and more distasteful to them, and they left the arrangement of the labour question to persons to whom the blacks were nothing, emancipated though they might be, except instruments of production. A negro can be attached to his employer as easily as a horse or dog. The horse or dog requires kind treatment, or he becomes indifferent or sullen ; so it is with the negro. But the forced equality of the races before the law made more difficult the growth of any kindly feeling. To the overseer on a plantation the black labourer was a machine out of which the problem was to get the maximum of work with the minimum of pay. In the slavery times the horse and dog relation was a real thing. The master and mistress joked and laughed with their dark bondsmen, knew Cæsar from Pompey, knew how many children each had, gave them small presents, cared for them when they were sick, and maintained them when they were old and past work. All this ended with emancipation."

"*All this ended with emancipation.*" Englishmen who desire to see their country's name no longer sullied, by such
things being possible under the flag, will be glad to think so.
Unfortunately, as Sir Anthony Musgrave justly points out, the
consequences of this degrading picture did not so easily end.
The children of "Pompey" and "Cæsar" had a marketable
value, and the masters and mistresses knew they could sell
them and make more money out of them than even by their
breed of horses and dogs. These slave-masters and -mistresses
discouraged the spread of Christianity among their blacks, and
would not permit them to learn to read. They also disliked
to see them go through the Christian ceremony of marriage,
because even in their eyes it would not then appear seemly to
forcibly separate children from parents, and husbands from
wives, by the hammer of the auctioneer. The parson of the
district was also sometimes a relative of the slave-owner, and
the solemn words "until death us do part, according to God's
holy ordinance" could not always be made a mockery of. The
dealer in men, therefore, had to care something for appearances.
He kept his people as animals, and hoped thus to avoid offend-
ing the instinct of every Christian community. But more will
be said of this in the chapter "Emancipation not Freedom."

In page 161 Mr. Froude says :—

"The poor black was a faithful servant as long as he was a slave. As
a freeman he is conscious of his inferiority at the bottom of his heart, and
would attach himself to a rational white employer with at least as much
fidelity as a spaniel. Like a spaniel, too, if he is denied the chance of
developing under guidance the better qualities which are in him, he will
drift back into a mangy cur."

He again says, page 348 :—

"In the English islands they are innocently happy in the unconscious-
ness of the obligations of morality. They eat, drink, sleep, and smoke,
and do the least in the way of work that they can. They have no ideas of
duty, and therefore are not made uneasy by neglecting it. One or other of
them occasionally rises in the legal or other profession, but there is no sign,
not the slightest, that the generality of the race are improving either in intelligence or moral habits ; all the evidence is the other way."

In these two typical passages—there are numerous others of
a similar nature throughout the book—Mr. Froude shows his
aims; he is not only attacking the black men, he attacks also

the Government for having liberated them from bondage. The Africans in the West Indies were improving while in slavery, according to him, but have lost ground since. This is the moral of Mr. Froude's fable—liberty is always bad.' We all know what the African slave was in the West Indies and how he was treated, and the subject need not be gone into here; something will be said about it, however, in the chapter "Emancipation not Freedom."

Englishmen who have forgotten all about the old horrors and abominations of slavery, and perhaps have never heard how the masters and mistresses were even more defiled by them than the people they held in bondage, may be unconsciously led into error by reading Mr. Froude's book. It will be proper therefore to bring forward some testimony of crushing weight to prove for the thousandth time, not only the falseness and unjustness of the charges of Mr. Froude, but their absurdity.

In the Report of the Royal Commissioners on the four Windward Islands—St. Vincent, Tobago, Grenada, St. Lucia—published in 1884, occurs the following :—

" We noticed everywhere signs of increasing popular prosperity, particularly in the generally acknowledged fact that the peasantry are better clothed and better housed than formerly. For instance, negro dwellings are now commonly roofed with shingles, and are generally in sound condition, a state of things said to be quite unknown twenty years ago. Instances were brought to our knowledge in which negro labourers had recently purchased land in small building plots at rates from £30 to £40 an acre."

What more could be said of the most prosperous peasantry in the most prosperous districts in Europe?

Speaking of the cultivation of cocoa, arrowroot, spices, and cotton in these four islands (as one colony), the Commissioners say : " The cultivation of these products is carried on to a very large extent, and especially in Grenada, by peasant proprietors, a flourishing class, who, as they increase in numbers, must greatly advance the general prosperity of the colony."

The total number of negro freeholders in the above islands of the above class, so highly spoken of, is at present at least 30,000. Consequent on this increase of tillage and industry the exports of the island of St. Lucia have trebled during the last thirty years.

That distinguished West Indian, the late Sir T. Graham Briggs, in a letter under date 28th January, 1883, says :—

"The recent improvement in Grenada is entirely due to the spread of cultivation of cocoa, which is principally due to the small holders of land, *i.e.*, the black labourers."

In another letter, dated 1st January, 1882, he says:—

"My father, who had by far the largest mind I ever met with in any West Indian, used always to tell me: Wherever any colony has not prospered, the fault lay, *not* with the labourers, but with the planters."

Mr. R. G. Haliburton, Q.C., a scion of one of our most distinguished colonial families, and himself a gentleman well known for his special knowledge of colonial questions, recently visited Jamaica for his health, and resided in the interior of the island, among the black and brown landholders, for nineteen months. Mr. Haliburton is, I believe, a Tory, but he states what he saw himself, and he frankly admits that what he did see entirely overthrew all his preconceived notions, which were somewhat after the pattern of Mr. Froude's, but by no means quite the same. Mr. Haliburton says:—

"On arriving at Jamaica, in search of sunshine and health, I was, in common with most persons who judge of the island from a distance, somewhat prejudiced against the black and brown people of that colony. I had been led to believe that they were fast relapsing into savages, and could not safely have a voice in their own affairs ; that firm, paternal sway was the only practical way of ruling them ; that, in consequence of their being able to acquire little holdings, either by purchase or by squatting, their tendency was to abjure work, raise a few yams and chickens, and steadily relapse into the state of listless African barbarism, from which their ancestors were torn by slave-hunters ; and that, whatever wages could be offered, they could not be induced to work on the sugar plantations—a field of labour which, therefore, must be abandoned, or entrusted to imported coolies ; in short, that labour was despised and abhorred by the blacks, as a survival of the horrors of slavery.

"I need hardly say that, having spent two winters in the island—my stay there extending to nineteen months—in the very districts where the black and brown people are generally small landowners, I found that my first impressions were most erroneous; that the people are willing and glad to work for a very scanty amount of wages ; and being small landowners has been a benefit to them ; and that they are in a singularly advanced state, considering their opportunities and their antecedents, and the evil influences and habits of former servitude. I found them very peaceable and law-abiding, and though given to small acts of prædial larceny (largely due to their lots of land being isolated and unprotected), they are generally very honest. For weeks I lived in a house, none of the doors of which were locked, or could be locked, for the keys had been lost. Poor people were, night and day, constantly coming to the place, and could have gone into the house and stolen articles of clothing, furniture, &c. Yet I never missed anything, and was told that my uneasiness as to the safety of my house was quite uncalled for. As a peasantry they compared favourably with the people of many of the countries which I have visited. Excepting occasionally meeting very poor people, I seldom saw persons in ragged clothes ; and their little houses, consisting sometimes of one, sometimes of three, but oftener of two rooms, were generally tidy and neat.

" Their holdings were small, ranging from two to ten acres, though some of the blacks owned large tracts. One intelligent and enterprising black man was a comparatively large landowner, and owned and bred many horses, cows, donkeys, and mules. The great ambition of the Jamaican black is to have a patch of land of his own, and when he succeeds in gratifying his land-hunger, he is thenceforth attached to the soil ; and, in many instances, neither sickness, nor want, nor even the fear of death itself, will tempt him to part with his land. The fact, too, that the blacks are in the habit (whether from choice or necessity I leave others to say) of burying their dead in their little holdings, may naturally intensify this feeling.

" It has been estimated that there are 60,000 landowners in Jamaica. Many who are too poor to buy land, or who live in districts where proprietors are unwilling to sell small lots to them, rent an acre or two. Many *penkeepers* (as owners of grazing estates are called) allow the blacks to clear and cultivate small tracts, which at the end of two years are sown in guinea grass and given up to the owners. Where 'the bush' is heavy, something is paid for clearing, and in other cases some small share of produce goes to the owners.

" I was surprised to find how many of the people could read and write ; and observed with pleasure the large number of decently-dressed children on their way to or from school."

The number of peasant proprietors in Jamaica is now somewhere about 60,000, and only for their industry the island would to-day be bankrupt. The large and rapidly increasing industry of fruit growth and export is practically in their hands. Indeed, every industry and every export has now chiefly to depend on them with the exception of the waning sugar industry. But even here they also do the most work, although it occupies only five per cent. of the population.

At a meeting of the Royal Colonial Institute, held on the 12th June, 1883, to hear a most valuable paper read by Mr. Morris—" Planting Enterprises in the West Indies "—a gentleman, during the discussion which followed, asked the Governor of Jamaica (Sir Anthony Musgrave), who was present, if he could throw any light as to what the people (meaning thereby the black population) were doing. Sir Anthony Musgrave answered : " I would say they were occupied in paying a greater part of the taxes."

Like testimony and of a character equally favourable to the blacks is abundant as regards the island of Trinidad, the Bahama Islands, and, in fact, everywhere in the West Indies. The movement is not confined to the British West Indies only, but extends to the Spanish, French, and others. The only exceptions seem to be the British Virgin Islands, so beautiful, so well placed, and so fertile by nature. Of these the Royal Commissioners said : " We found, for instance, that charcoal-burners and stock-breeders in the Virgin Islands were leaving them for neighbouring foreign possessions, simply in order to escape the heavy export duties the government in the English colony levied on all charcoal and stock exported." These charcoal-burners and stock-breeders are all black men. It would have been difficult, nay, impossible, to mismanage a place more than the Virgin Islands have been mismanaged. " The English in the West Indies " left them to their fate years ago, and now the British black man is himself obliged to give them up, for even he can make nothing of them.

These are the people Mr. Froude would have us believe are only fitted at best for a modified condition of slavery. Who can read all this testimony alongside of Mr. Froude's assertions and not see how completely he is misleading his readers ? Nothing is easier than to write a book against a people, and if these people happen to be lowly born, of no rank in the world's history, children of misfortune, and the sport of adverse fates, why, the thing can be done without anyone even suspecting that it is not all truth. Then there is the worldly prejudice which always exists against such people. We are all told how wrong it is to have this prejudice, but it exists nevertheless. Some amongst us try to combat the feeling and make efforts to be generous. Others feed the prejudice, and prejudice has ever found its chiefest nourishment in calumny. To this it lends a ready ear. The British black man does not ask for any commiseration ; he does not require it. He does not ask for generosity even ; he can do without it. But he cannot do without justice. None of us can.

What then is the present position of the African races or British black men in the West Indies ? They are the chief inhabitants ; the whites in Trinidad are less than six per cent.

of the population, in Barbados they are under eight and a
half per cent., in Antigua they are under five and a quarter per
cent., in Jamaica they are under two and a half per cent.; in
none of the other West Indian islands, except the Bahamas,
do they muster two per cent. of the population. In British
Guiana they are under one and a half per cent., and less still
in Honduras, on the mainland of South America. In the
Bahamas the white blood is reckoned to be about one-fifth.

In all the islands, including the Bahamas, the more or less
cultivated land is said to be about 1,550,000 acres, out of a
total of over 6,000,000 acres. The population numbers about
1,250,000. The average exports may be put at £6,000,000,
and the imports at something under this figure. A total import and export trade of nearly £12,000,000. The revenue
raised is equal to about £1,444,000. The area of British
Guiana is now said to be 109,000 square miles, and Honduras
7,500 square miles; the population of these two mainland
colonies is about 300,000. Their exports have been over
£2,800,000 in value, and their imports about £2,000,000
yearly; the revenue of the two colonies is under £500,000.
The value of exports has recently fallen, and imports have
been affected in a like proportion.

It is the black men who pay the taxes and who support
Her Majesty's Government. In the islands, especially, it is
the black men who are taking up the land and cultivating it.
They are rapidly becoming peasant proprietors after the
European type. It is the black men who do nearly all the
labour. The West Indies are essentially agricultural, but the
black men make very good mechanics, and skilful and bold
sailors, and they do well mostly all the work that has to be
done this way. In times of trouble and difficulty they are
found to be reliable soldiers, and a couple or three regiments
of Mr. Froude's black men help very materially to keep the
flag of England from being thought too slightingly of on the
West Coast of Africa.

Nowhere, not even in England itself, are people to be
met with more law-abiding or more loyal to the Crown than
the British black men. They know one thing: that it is the
people of England that sounded the tocsin of freedom for
their race. No! not even the bitter words of Mr. Froude, not
all his efforts to humiliate and degrade them in the eyes of

their fellow-subjects, can alter this sentiment. They believe now and they will continue to believe, and they will be justified in believing, that the people of England will never turn back from the great act of supreme justice in emancipation. They believe, and they are justified in believing, that England will do more; England from time to time will give them that just measure of liberty in self-government to which their efforts and position and loyal character entitle them.

But the British black men must remember this, they have many faults. Most of these faults were forced on them by slavery, doubtless, but they are faults nevertheless. This book of Mr. Froude's should be a warning to them—a warning how ready some are to re-forge their chains. They must work and struggle to merit that freedom no man can truly be said to possess who has not true knowledge—true Christian knowledge, and the knowledge how to work and labour. Let the leaders among the black men get their sons to be surveyors, men of science and men of action, and not look so much to be lawyers and place-hunters. Let them learn and take up industries. They are as competent to do all this as they show themselves now to be competent to become able lawyers, able medical men, and able ministers of religion. A race of men to be valuable must contain within its ranks the main elements of human progress. A man must not believe only, he must also work. They are accused of slothfulness, and to some extent they merit the blame. But those who know the Africans and their descendants the British black men can truly say they are competent to break away from this slothfulness and be true men.

> ". . . . . . What is a man,
> If his chief good, and market of his time,
> Be but to sleep and feed? A beast, no more.
> Sure, He, that made us with such large discourse,
> Looking before and after, gave us not
> That capability and Godlike reason,
> To fust in us unused."

CHAPTER VI.

EMANCIPATION NOT FREEDOM.

SPEAKING of Barbados, page 105, Mr. Froude says: "The great prosperity of the island ended with emancipation." How came Mr. Froude to say this, unless his notion of prosperity differs from that of other people ? The exports have largely increased, the imports have largely increased, and the population has increased from about 800 to over 1,000 to the square mile. The movements of trade have increased, and the wages of labour have increased. The value of sugar has gone down, but this is not owing to emancipation, while the number of sugar works on the island has increased by fifty per cent. The revenue and expenditure have, of course, also greatly increased, but everyone will agree with Mr. Froude if he deems this in itself no sure indication of prosperity. The testimony of those who know the island well goes to show the people to be more than ten times better educated than before emancipation, while every other indication of a higher-class civilisation in all ranks of life has shown an equal advance. The prosperity Mr. Froude regrets was that of some of the slave-owners, several of whom were already virtually bankrupt when emancipation was decreed.

A well-known West Indian gentleman, whose recent death has been a great loss to these colonies, Sir Thomas Graham Briggs, of Barbados and Nevis, in a letter dated May 3, 1882, says :—

" My father was the only man I *knew* who had favoured the freedom of labour in Barbados before it was brought about ; but there were a few, a very few others ; and now I do not believe that you could find more than ten per cent. of the landowners who would return to it, or who do not see the advantage of free over slave labour. But although this is so, there is still the curse of old ideas and old habits, which, unconsciously often,

warps their ideas and their actions from what is right and best even for
their class. . . . I have long maintained that whenever a West Indian
island is not prosperous, the main fault lies not with the labourers but
with the planters who have not been equal to cope with the new order of
things."

This is from a gentleman Mr. Froude justly designates the
most distinguished representative of the old Barbadian families,
himself one of the largest cultivators in the West Indies, and
the son and grandson of men eminent in their day.

Had it not been for emancipation, Barbados would have
been soon ruined about that time, and not only Barbados but
all the other British West Indies. It is necessary to explain
here a well-known fact which Mr. Froude never heard of—his
informants judiciously kept it from him. If Mr. Froude heard
of it, he wisely says nothing about it. This is the damning
fact : *the slaves were dying off.* This is a fact as well known
and as well proven as any fact in history. It is not necessary
to multiply proofs of this truth. This is what Sir Anthony
Musgrave, the then Governor of Jamaica, said, in a letter to the
Times, Sept. 1, 1883, I have already had occasion to quote
from :—

"The fact is that the abolition of slavery led to the increase of the
population, which it is well known was fast dying out previously, in
Jamaica, at all events, after the cessation of the slave trade, and retarded
the collapse, which was inevitable. . . . The compensation money paid
for the slaves at the time of emancipation afforded an artificial stimulus,
which galvanised into temporary vitality a social and agricultural system
already moribund."

Mr. Froude makes an incorrect statement, and he builds
on this a superstructure as unsound as such things usually are.
Slavery can never be kept up anywhere without fresh supplies
of imported men, women, and children. When the conscience
of England revolted against the atrocities of export slavery from
Africa, the knell of slavery was sounded in the West Indies.
We all know how hard it is for truth, justice, and honour to
triumph when cupidity and avarice stop the way. Slavery died
hard in the West Indies. No miser ever clung to his money-
bags with a greater tenacity of purpose than did the planters to
slavery. But the money-bags are after all the poor miser's
own. But the slaves held in bondage were God's creatures
stolen from their country and their homes.

Slavery was only kept alive in Cuba by export slavery being carried on, despite of treaties, with all the horrors of the middle passage. An Emancipation Act was passed for the possessions of Spain when it became evident that no more slaves were to be had even this way.

The slaves were dying off. After emancipation the now emancipated blacks began to increase in number, in all the British West Indies, until this increase was again somewhat checked by the dearness of food caused by the heavy duties levied at the ports on imported food-stuffs.

Another very incorrect statement of Mr. Froude is made in page 121, as follows :—

"The blacks whom, in a fit of virtuous benevolence, we emancipated, do not feel they are particularly obliged to us. They think, if they think at all, that they were ill-treated originally, and have received no more than was due to them, and that perhaps it was not benevolence at all on our part, but a desire to free ourselves from the reproach of slave-holding."

The people of this generation are apt to forget the reasons that led to the Act of Emancipation. Everyone will admit these reasons were probably complex. We have not always Wilberforces amongst us to teach us our duty, and the name of this great Englishman may be nigh forgotten in England. Among the black people of that part of Western Africa where we had our chief slave preserves, among the liberated at Sierra Leone and other places, and in all our West Indies, there is the figure of one great Englishman, well known, ever revered ; that figure is Wilberforce. In all his book Mr. Froude does not mention this name once. But Mr. Froude's book is both a pæan and a dirge; he sings the triumphs of slavery, and he weeps over its fall. Little likely, therefore, that the name of this apostle of freedom should find a place there. Nothing that he said in his book, so crowded with misleading statements, could surpass in inexactitude the above statement, and it demonstrates how completely he has misread the British black man. The reasons of Englishmen for decreeing freedom were complex ; some did it from Christian principle, some from a native generosity of character, some from a dislike to see the name of England dishonoured, some from motives of policy, some from expediency. But the black man never looked the gift horse in the mouth. He knew who originated the movement, and he knew who carried it to a successful issue. To him Wilberforce means England. This is why the British black man is so loyal and so true. He sees the greatness and generosity of England personified in a name dear to English-men and to the world. It is well for England and for English-men that such a grand character emblemises the nation among the black races that acknowledge and follow the flag. The black man deems himself deeply beholden to England, it may be more so than she deserves. Mr. Froude knows his country-men better than the British black man does. The paragraph from his book above quoted is probably Mr. Froude's own opinion. It is certainly not that of the British black man.

No Englishman of weight, whatever he may have privately thought, has become the apologist of slavery in recent times. Mr. Froude's book, however, is a justification for slavery. He justifies it for three reasons : the first reason is that the African by becoming a West Indian slave escaped from a worse fate in his own country ; the second reason is that the treatment he received in the West Indies as a slave was of advantage to him ; the third reason is that since emancipation he has been deteriorating.

It is impossible for Mr. Froude to have found out all this in his couple of months' sojourn, for two reasons : the first reason is that he knows nothing of the countries where the slaves came from, and therefore he could know nothing of the internal conditions of such countries ; the second reason is that he was not in a position, and had neither the necessary time nor the opportunities, to study the British black men in the West Indies.

Mr. Froude's opinion is, therefore, either the old hackneyed one of the apologists for slavery in times gone by served up afresh, or, what is more probable, it is an opinion simply thrust forward for the purpose of giving some body to an argument which otherwise would collapse for want of one.

This is what Mr. Froude says, page 235 :—

" Slavery was a survival from a social order which has passed away, and slavery could not be continued. It does not follow *per se* that it was a crime. The negroes who were sold to the dealers in the African factories were most of them either slaves already to worse masters or were *servi*, servants in the old meaning of the word, prisoners of war, or else criminals, *servati*, or reserved from death. They would otherwise have been killed ;

and, since the slave trade has been abolished, are again killed in the two celebrated 'customs.' It was a crime when the chiefs made war on each other for the sake of captives whom they could turn into money. In many instances, perhaps in most, it was innocent and even beneficent."

In pages 246-7 he says, speaking of the blacks in a country hamlet :—

"The men touched their hats respectfully (as they eminently did not in Kingston and its environs). The women smiled and curtsied, and the children looked shy when one spoke to them.

"The name of slavery is a horror to us ; but there must have been something human and kindly about it, too, when it left upon the character the marks of courtesy and good breeding. I wish I could say as much for the effect of modern ideas. The negroes in Mandeville were, perhaps, as happy in their old condition as they have been since their glorious emancipation ; and some of them to this day speak regretfully of a time when children did not die of neglect ; when the sick and aged were taken care of, and the strong and healthy were, at least, as well looked after as their owner's cattle.

"Slavery could not last ; but neither can the condition last which has followed it. The equality between black and white is a forced equality and not a real one, and Nature in the long run has her way, and readjusts in their proper relations what theorists and philanthropists have disturbed."

In page 348 he says :—

"The blacks as long as they were slaves were docile and partially civilised. They have behaved on the whole well in our island since emancipation, for though they were personally free the whites were still their rulers, and they looked up to them with respect. They have acquired land and notions of property, some of them can read, many of them are tolerable workmen, and some excellent, but in character the movement is backwards, not forwards."

The above statements are very remarkable. In the first one Mr. Froude assumes against every evidence that the people captured and exported as slaves were all of a servile order in their own country. Did Mr. Froude never read in the books of Livingstone, Stanley, Cameron, and a dozen others, of the exploits of Tippoo Tib and such-like Arab slave-hunters, and the awful desolation they cause in Africa, and the barbarities they commit on defenceless men, women, and children ? Multiply these recorded authenticated facts a hundredfold, and we have a picture of the merciful slavery of Mr. Froude in the great days of export slavery. Africa is no more made up of Dahomeys than Europe is made up of King Bombas. It is the very perversion of history to state what Mr. Froude states. Among the exported slaves there were probably a few criminals and maybe some domestic slaves, but the majority are well known to have been men, women, and children captured in war.   It is also well known that wars were carried on for the express object of getting slaves for export.   It is also well known that these wars were not ordinary wars, but were wars of extermination, of depopulation of whole districts; the object being not to gain mastery of a country to rule it, but to carry off the inhabitants for sale.

The second statement of Mr. Froude, pp. 246-7, may partially be answered by another extract from his book.   In page 40 he describes the bondage of the old days in Barbados : " There were 60,000 slaves who would rebel if they saw a hope of success.   They were ill-fed, hard-driven.   On the least symptom of insubordination they were killed without mercy ; sometimes they were burnt alive, or hung up in iron cages to die."   The above is Labat's account accepted by Mr. Froude. This Labat was a noted traveller in his day, and there is no reason to suspect his testimony.   It also appears from the same authority that recently imported negroes often destroyed themselves, in the belief that when dead they would return to their own country.   The bodies of these suicides were exposed in iron cages in the English and French islands, to convince the poor slaves that even by death they did not escape.   Truly an improving form of life for the African ! When more merciful times arrived, later on, and slaves were treated more as valuable cattle—as " Pompey " and " Cæsar " —no doubt the Froudes of the period found the change to be dangerous to the State, and fraught with demoralising consequences to the blacks themselves.

If Mr. Froude's description of the African, both under British bondage and since he has been freed, be not all imagination and conjecture, it shows conclusively that the form of slavery the Africans underwent must have been the most degrading and demoralising known in the history of mankind. Better far for a man to have been a captive reserved for the bloody customs of Dahomey than to have been a slave after Mr. Froude's West Indian pattern—a mere animal, and the breeder of animals.

How utterly unlike the truth are Mr. Froude's statements

about slavery in Africa itself, everyone who knows anything of the country can testify. As a general rule, domestic slaves are not saleable at all ; their sale is not permitted by local laws and customs. Domestic and agricultural slaves in Africa are, at their worst, as well off as the serfs were in Russia. The number of free men in Africa is also greater than the number of serfs. In the slave-hunting, slave-exporting days, every man captured was shipped, whether he happened to be a chief or a serf.

As regards the customs of Dahomey and Ashanti, no one would care to do aught but deplore them. Can Mr. Froude name any one other place in all Africa where these customs exist to a like extent, or anything near it ? Dahomey and Ashanti are small places indeed compared to all Africa. Besides, a study of this question will show that human sacrifices existed in Western Africa, at places, before the export slavery commenced, but that they became afterwards intensified, due to the recklessness for human life engendered by the slave-hunts and the encouragement given by slave-dealers. In fact, the whole of the brutality of Dahomey and Ashanti, and nearly all the wars and disorganisation so apparent along the Western African coast and inland, can be distinctly traced to the teachings of the export slave-dealers.

The gentle manners of the bucolic black men, which so struck Mr. Froude at Mandeville, in Jamaica, in comparison with the indifference of their Kingston brothers, is of a kind not uncommon in England itself. Strangers—even if they be Mr. Froude's—do not look to be saluted in the streets of Hull or Bristol, but in a country lane such things are not impossible. Good manners are not always a true indication of a superior civilisation, or even of moral excellence, but everyone is glad to meet with them. The manners of the British black men are much open to improvement. They have greatly improved since emancipation.

Everyone admits the children of the slaves were not permitted to die of neglect—"they were as well looked after as the owner's cattle." They were not fatted for the butcher, but they were fatted for the auction mart, and to be stalwart enough to support the knout of the overseer. But man is a mysterious creature. The mightiest intellects of the world have been studying him and theorising about him ever since those remote ages when men first turned to inquire what they themselves might be.   One of the yet unexplained mysteries concerning man is the disappearance of certain races, while other races subjected to the same or similar conditions survive.   The negro well fed and cared for as an animal began to die out rapidly in the West Indies ; with freedom and intermittent starvation he survives and multiplies.   There are many races that have died out of the world leaving no mark of their passage, or only traces almost as impalpable as shadows ; the process may be seen to-day in full operation with the red man, the Maories, and the Polynesians.   Other races, like the Jews, have dispersed and live on as separate communities, and refuse to die out anywhere, after being subjected to every condition that makes for extinction.   Whatever the negro else may be he, is destined to be one of the survivals.   He will live in the world of the future.   This is a fact which must not be lost sight of.

Mr. Froude says above :—

" Slavery could not last ; but neither can the condition last which has followed it.   The equality between black and white is a forced equality and not a real one, and Nature in the long run has her way, and readjusts in their proper relations what theorists and philanthropists have disturbed."

What does Mr. Froude mean by this passage ?   Every man is entitled to have an opinion of his own on nearly any subject, but if he delivers it as a universally accepted truism he must expect to see it scrutinised.

The French chalk up on their prisons the words " *Liberté, égalité, fraternité*," just as they do on any other public buildings.   At first sight the words might seem somewhat out of place, but they are not ; they are as appropriate on the prison wall as on the façade of the Chamber of Deputies.   The three words may mean a great deal indeed.   When they apply to the State in reference to the individual, that all are equal before it and before the law, they are then appropriate everywhere.   If they mean that all men are individually equal to one another, are equally free, or are brothers in one another's eyes, they are nonsense anywhere, from every point of view except that of pure religion.

In practical life, therefore, the contention of Mr. Froude is right enough, if kept within its proper limits.   It is right in the

West Indies with reference to the majority of the blacks and the whole of the " mean " whites *vis-à-vis* the white aristocracy of the islands. It is equally true everywhere where society contains an aristocratic element. In the aristocratic Roman Republic it was particularly conspicuous by the impassable barriers drawn between patricians and plebs.

What is therefore the " condition " of the British black man in the West Indies which has resulted from emancipation, and which Mr. Froude thinks cannot last? Philanthropists have " disturbed" nothing in these islands but the old slavery. It looks at first sight very much as if Mr. Froude thought slavery itself should be reintroduced, either in its old or in some mitigated form. There is and can be no equality in the West Indies except it be *vis-à-vis* the state and the law. Social equality is a question for society to decide, and no state laws have ever been able to successfully battle with its decrees. Society, especially English society, can be safely left to take care of itself. The poor labourer, black or white, is never likely to be regarded on a footing of equality. But a very, very rich black man, one who had carriages, horses, and diamonds, might have a chance, who knows? Do we deem Chinamen our social equals? or even Hindoo princes for that matter? and yet the Chinese Empire is a growing power in the world, and Hindoo princes are people of much political importance.

What are the social, legal, and political rights possessed by the British black man that are deemed so insupportable by our fastidious white brothers in the West Indies? They are allowed to dress as they please, to acquire land if they pay for it, and to supply the Queen's government with most of the taxes. They are allowed to starve and to remain uneducated. If they are clever enough or rich enough they may acquire a commensurate social standing among their fellows. They can be policemen, soldiers (rank and file), and may hold offices of trust in the local state. They are ministers of religion, schoolmasters, barristers, and doctors. Since the abolition of slavery 140,000 of them have become peasant proprietors, and perhaps 10,000 more are men of considerable property and comparative wealth. They practically do all the labour and supervising of labour that is done in these colonies. They are railway engineers, stokers, sailors, and mechanics

Socially, what would the islands be without them? That is the question. And if society cannot exist without their aid and help, why not allow them the fruits of their exertions?

Is it the legal rights of the blacks that are repugnant to Mr. Froude's whites? They have only those rights before the law every British subject enjoys.

It is probably political rights that Mr. Froude refers to. He would give the white man a vote, but would not give one to a black man ; or, more likely, he would not give either of them one. Just now no one, either black or white, has any political rights worth talking about except at Barbados, to a very limited extent in Jamaica, and in the Bahamas where it is neutralised for good. But we all know Mr. Froude is not favourable to granting any political rights whatever to the West Indian people. He wants the East Indian system. He wants no assemblies, no voting. He wants a pure bureaucratic rule in all things, directed by a London council. But in this case things would remain pretty nearly as they are now. The East Indian system and the present system of West Indian rule would practically, with one or two exceptions, only amount to a difference in name.

But although the words of Mr. Froude above quoted have no meaning when analysed, they are well calculated to breed mischief in the West Indies. The British black men may read in them a wish on the part of the whites to return to a servile or a semi-servile condition for the black population. It ought to be plainly said at once that any attempt in that direction would lead to a racial war—a social war with its undying hatreds. Let there be no mistake ; the British black men are loyal and true to the flag of England, but any signs to retake what has been granted would be fatal to these colonies.

Properly weighed, these hasty words of Mr. Froude would be a justification to the Haytians for all their evil and foolish acts. If whites and blacks cannot live alongside one another in the same country without the domination of the former over the latter being certain ultimately to result, why, the blacks would be only using common prudence in expelling the whites!

There is another solution. Do the British black men desire to be ruled and governed by the local whites? They do not ; what is more, the local whites do not desire this either. Do the British black men desire to govern themselves? They do not. But both whites and blacks desire a reasonable measure of local self-government, both races having equal rights.

If Mr. Froude's words are meant to convey the meaning that whites and blacks are not socially equal, no one will quarrel with him. The British black man will be the social equal of the white if, by his own exertions, he makes himself so, but certainly not otherwise. No law can make men equal. There was no law passed in the West Indies with this object in view, and neither "theorists" nor "philanthropists" have yet shown any desire to pass any such law.

But theorists and philanthropists have very much objected to slavery, and the most practical men the world has ever yet seen are of one mind with them in this. They deem slavery was bad for the slave, but worse, much worse, in its demoralising effects on the master; therefore they will have none of it. All that was done in the West Indies for the black man was simply to break his chains and let him go free. "The condition that has followed" slavery is, in Mr. Froude's opinion, as little likely to last as slavery itself. It is to be hoped the present condition will not last. A distinct movement in advance is now a necessary corollary from emancipation.

Emancipation was a necessity. The ordinary freedom of British subjects everywhere to supervise their local administration, and the raising and expenditure of their local revenues, has now become a necessity of the first order in the West Indies. This is the freedom Mr. Froude would not have England grant; emancipation cannot be withdrawn, he admits, but he would not give freedom.

There is nothing to be gained by anyone in exalting a man above his merits, and the same reasoning applies to a people. The British black men as a body have many grave faults of conduct and many serious deficiencies in character. But then, we must remember, they were slaves only about fifty years ago. Besides, we have no right to measure them alongside Englishmen. There are some excellent people entirely white, and who were never slaves, who would look diminutive enough in the process. But, although the British black men have many faults of character, this much can be fairly said for them: they have made marvellous good use of the opportunities—the very few opportunities—that have been put in their way. This is all the proof practical men want to enable them to decide whether a people are really fitted for the rights of citizens. The British black men having, on the whole, answered this test question affirmatively, no more in fairness should be required of them.

CHAPTER VII.

THE crying evil of the West Indies is said to be want of labour. There is some truth in this, but the usual complaints one hears are misleading. Labour, like every other force in nature, requires intelligent handling or the results will be disappointing. For all practical purposes the African man is the only labour-force available in the West Indies. This man is admitted to be the animal embodiment of all that can be desired as a labourer. There are enough men of his race in the British West Indies to carry on five times the present cultivation without any strain. This labour is not properly utilised because the wages given are too low and food, due to taxation of imports, is too dear. The African man is one of the largest feeders in the human family ; this, perhaps, is why he is so strong physically. Mr. E. P. Pearce Edgcumbe, LL.D., relates, in a book of his published last year by Chatto and Windus, an anecdote connected with a coffee estate near Rio in Brazil. It appears there were a number of African slaves employed who apparently worked, or were made to work, fairly well. But the estate, which is the property of a company, did not pay. As the soil was everything that could be desired, no one could understand why it failed. After many changes it was eventually determined to get an American overseer, because Americans have the reputation of making a thing pay where other men cannot. This overseer after a time doubled the food rations of his men. After a further time he again doubled them. In course of time, therefore, this American overseer found it advisable to quadruple the food rations of his labourers. Since this change the returns from the estate have been remunerative. The old managers tried to get up steam without burning fuel. This is the secret of West Indian failures; the labourers, at present wages and present prices for food, cannot get enough to eat. It is a very simple reason, but it is one that some people obstinately refuse to see.

The Royal Commission that reported on certain West Indian islands in 1884 gave a mass of evidence which went to show that the blacks did not work anything like as much as they could. There was a greater weight of evidence in their favour. There was proof everywhere that the black men were willing to leave their island homes to go where good wages were to be had—sufficient to leave a margin wherewith to save. On the whole, the evidence made it apparent that, in some of the islands, at all events, there were many circumstances at work to discourage a naturally hardworking and thrifty man, and the lazy, the thriftless, and the naturally indolent, had many things in their favour. The partisans of either view of the black labourer—that he was capricious, unreliable and lazy, or that he was hardworking and easily managed—have materials at hand to support their contentions. The impartially-minded will conclude that wherever industry is doubtfully encouraged and not adequately rewarded, the opposing forces will more or less flourish, whatever may be the colour of the population. This is the true position of the labour question in the West Indies. The black is apt to be a lazy fellow in that island where he is little or none the better for working hard. When wages are high, or where extra money beyond daily wants may be earned, many labourers save up money and buy land. This tends to withdraw the best class of labour. It is the same process which daily goes on in Australia and Canada, and our black West Indians cannot be blamed for using the like privileges and opportunities.

The Report of the Royal Commission appointed in 1882 to inquire into the public revenues, expenditure, debts, and liabilities of certain West Indian islands, including Jamaica, was published, as stated above, in 1884. The Commissioners landed in Jamaica on the 5th January, 1883. They left the island on the 25th February. Their statements about labour are, of course, consistent with much of the printed evidence, but it is the evidence of planters and others, whose utterances for years are well known to have been hostile to the black population. On the whole, the report runs counter to the evidence of impartial men and the general facts that leak out from time to time. In this, as in some other matters, this report is a planter's report. As the London *Times* remarked at the time, the Commissioners had evidently been surrounded by those subtle influences by which men always get surrounded on such occasions if not well on their guard, and the poor black labourers were, consequently, nowhere ; they never had a chance of justice being done them.

In page 87 of their Jamaican Report, the Commissioners re-tell the old tale : that labourers will only work three or four hours a day, and then only on four days a week, and then comes the whole object of the preamble : East Indian coolies, under an indenture to work for planters for five years, are to be introduced, partly at the public cost.

This Report of the two Commissioners on this matter of labour is in direct opposition to, and is wholly and entirely irreconcilable with, facts patent to every one who impartially inquires. That the blacks are not as good labourers as they might easily be made, that they do not work as much or as well as every one desires they should, is undoubted ; but the causes for this are the low wages offered, combined with the dear food. Thousands of these labourers, it has been seen, emigrate to get good wages elsewhere, at the imminent risk of their lives, and thousands more make good peasant cultivators. The Report of the Royal Commission, with respect to this matter of labour, fails entirely to grasp the situation.

Mr. Laborde, the Administrator of the Island of Tobago, in his evidence before the Royal Commissioners, said : " Labour is driven out of the island ; in crop time they get employment ; out of crop the planters will not employ them."

The Island of St. Vincent, as regards peasant holdings, is an exception to the other Windward Islands. It appears that much of the land here is a monopoly, but the labour supply is none the better for that. Mr. Gore, the Lieutenant-Governor, said in his evidence: "There are very few small holdings; planters will rent, but not sell. The planters want to keep the people absolutely dependent on them." He said that two-thirds of the island belonged to a company.

At the Island of St. Lucia, the agent for the Royal Mail Packet Company said : " People were leaving fast for Colon (Panama), sixty, seventy, and eighty going by each steamer."

The Colonial Secretary, Mr. Meagher, said : " Labour is very hard to get; wages are 1s. 4d. for men, 1s. for women. The majority of the labourers squat. The people are law-abiding." The labourers themselves, when questioned by the Commissioners, said that they had not enough work, and were insufficiently paid for the work they did. They said 10d. a day was the wage.

The evidence taken before the Royal Commissioners at the Island of Dominica showed that the chief estates gave only three days' work a week, and yet planters loudly complained that labourers could not be relied on for giving consecutive work. It was evident the three things wanted in this island were capital, enterprise, and " go," and that the cause of its backwardness is the practical absence of all three. Mr. Fadelle, Registrar and Provost-Marshal, a forty years' resident, said : " We have a number of independent small owners of land ; one-seventh of the sugar and almost all the cocoa exported from here are produced by this class of planters." He said that nearly all the towns and villages belonged to the artisan, shopkeeping, and labouring classes. Considerable quantities of ground provisions are grown, and the importations of foodstuffs are, therefore, greatly less than in the islands farther north ; the commercial movement in this direction is, consequently, also absent. Mr. Fadelle said that if a sugar estate cannot be profitably cultivated it is not for want of labour ; that the soil of Dominica, except in a very few estates, cannot be made to yield a paying quantity of sugar.

We are here getting at the truth. The growing of the right crop for the climate and soil, and its intelligent cultivation, is what is needed in Dominica. No amount of the best labour will avail if a product is selected that can never yield a marketable result. Nearly everything that grows in the tropics will grow in Dominica ; but sugar, on the whole, gives a poor yield. Nevertheless, the cultivation of no other product has yet been attempted on a scale sufficiently large to appreciably mend the fortunes of this colony, so splendidly endowed by nature.

Mr. Froude says of the black people of Dominica : " They are excellent boatmen, excellent fishermen, excellent mechanics, ready to undertake any work if treated with courtesy and kindness." He met a successful planter of limes and coffee—

Dr. Nicholls—who praised his black labourers. Dr. Nicholls asked Mr. Froude why young Englishmen preferred Ceylon and Borneo while they had an island like Dominica within a fortnight's sail of Plymouth. Mr. Froude thinks the explanation lies in the tendencies of English policy to the black population, and "that a local government created by representatives of the negro vote would make a residence there for an energetic and self-respecting European less tolerable than in any other part of the globe." Mr. Froude's aspect of the question is certainly original; no one ever heard of it before either in Dominica or in any other of the West Indian colonies, or, indeed, anywhere else. Since Dominica has been a British colony it has been paternally and bureaucratically ruled from a Downing Street office, and there consequently never existed any local government created by a negro or any other vote. The young Englishman who could fear the faint shadow of a local government of such a place would have been but a poor fellow at best, and would have made a sorry colonist anywhere. This is one of those misleading statements of Mr. Froude, so much to be regretted. Dr. Nicholls was himself the best proof of the unsoundness of Mr. Froude's hypothesis. He lived in the colony, and evidently thought there was no valid reason for Englishmen not doing as he did. Mr. Froude's object is to discourage any possible tendency in the Colonial Office to give something more of self-government to these colonies, and perhaps even to discredit that poor phantom of self-government even now possessed by Dominica in its powerless chamber. It is refreshing to hear no one say of this island that its want of success has been due to the resident blacks, although these latter obviously do not make as much of their means and opportunities as they well might.

Dominica was the only one of the Confederated Leeward Islands visited by Mr. Froude. He hints they are all after the same pattern, and that the description of the people of one answers for all. No greater error could possibly be made. Antigua, St. Kitts, and Nevis differ from Dominica as much as climate and nature of soil, and the language, religion, and perhaps even race of the inhabitants, can make differences. To Mr. Froude, who knows nothing of Africa, every African is the same—a Mandingo, a Yollof, a Krooman, a Fantee, an

Aku, an Ebo, the countless tribes of the interior, and a native of the Congo, are one. Yet the racial differences between these people are wider than the same differences between Europeans. There is no doubt that the various African races we sent as slaves to the West Indies have more or less amalgamated there. But, nevertheless, it is obvious to everyone who cares to examine this interesting problem that important distinctions do exist between the people of the several islands. Mr. Froude somewhere says the black West Indians looked all as similar to him as a flock of sheep did. This peculiarity of vision has been often remarked of people who are unfamiliar with an object. But not to insist too much on this point, it will perhaps be enough to say that Antigua, St. Kitts, and Nevis are islands where, on the whole, the people are Protestants and speak English, and that in Dominica the people are Catholic and speak a French patois, Dominica is a mountainous island, loaded with forests to the clouds, with an unfailing rainfall. Antigua, St. Kitts, and Nevis are, at the most, hilly, are but slightly forested, and are very liable to droughts. St. Kitts also differs from all the other above-mentioned islands in a very important respect; the whole of the land worth cultivating is under cultivation. Labourers were leaving the island of Nevis for Trinidad and also for the gold mines of Venezuela. The picturesque little island of Montserrat and the Virgin group are also in the present Leeward Confederacy. The former is well known from its lime-juice. It is almost a pity the Virgin Islands are not a dependency of Hayti instead of Great Britain. Had they been so we should have had a magnificent page or two from Mr. Froude to demonstrate the low depths to which the fortunes of such a promising group of islands could be reduced by the unchecked mismanagement of a government of black men. The one policeman in the group, it was hinted, was himself a smuggler. In the report of the Royal Commissioners there was no evidence forthcoming against the black labourers in any of the Leeward Islands. Some said labour was plentiful, and some that it was scarce, but no one that it was dear or that it was bad.

The labour question in Jamaica has always been the most prominent topic with respect to that island. The evidence taken by the Royal Commission, 1883-4, was more conflicting than was the case in any other island. The Commissioners themselves inclined to the belief that the blacks did not work satisfactorily, and that planters and estate owners could not depend on them. It was made clear, however, that this condition of things was due not to the inherent lazy qualities of the blacks, but to want of sufficient inducements to labour. The labouring blacks were leaving the island in thousands for Panama, where they knew many of their number would die, for the sake of the high wages obtained there which would enable those who survived to return and buy a plot of land of their own. Over 20,000 of them have done this. People who do this kind of thing possess qualities which could, and should, be utilised at home. To do Mr. Froude justice, he does not speak against the African as a labourer. Indeed, it would be difficult to do so in the West Indies. Mr. Froude even sometimes praises him—as a labourer. All the labour that is done in the island is his doing except some of the sugar-growing, which is done by gangs of East Indian coolies.

When properly analysed the whole evidence shows that it is not so much the amount as the distribution of labour that is complained of. The white planter thinks it the duty of the black labourer to work only for him, and at low wages, and that it is the business of Government so to legislate as to bring this about. Mr. Froude said Colonel J., commanding the garrison of Jamaica (who was acting as Governor temporarily while Mr. Froude was in the island),

"confirmed the complaint which I had heard so often that the blacks would not work for wages more than three days in the week, or regularly upon these, preferring to cultivate their own yams and sweet potatoes; but as it was admitted that they did work one way or another at home, I could not see that there was much to complain of. The blacks were only doing as we do. We, too, only work as much as we like or as we must, and we prefer working for ourselves to working for others."

It is more than likely Colonel J. had not a profound knowledge of the labour question. But he succeeded in confirming the complaint Mr. Froude had so often heard that the blacks would not work regularly for even three days a week. Mr. Froude, however, having no political object to gain by accentuating this charge against the Jamaican blacks, justifies them. But the charge is not altogether true. The regular labouring blacks of Jamaica are glad enough to get permanent work and steady, fair wages.

But there is no doubt that people who have to exist solely by labouring for others are becoming scarcer. The peasant proprietors are greatly increasing in number yearly, and they are entirely recruited from among the most thrifty and hard-working black labourers. A small peasant proprietor is willing to hire himself to a planter for very moderate wages, but, obviously, his labour cannot be continuous or always available because he has his own plot to look after. People who condemn so readily the British black man for being lazy do so in ignorance of facts. The cultivation of sugar-cane requires almost a man an acre. With slave labour or with coolie labour a planter has his hands always resident on the estate, because he is bound by law to keep them all the year round, whether he requires their labour for the whole period or not. With free labour it is different ; the planter reduces the number of hands at certain seasons, when it suits him to do so ; he is angry if the discharged blacks do not all immediately respond to his call when crop time comes round. On the other hand, the black labourers, to obviate the probability of being starved during the months the planter does not want them, are disposed to seek other means of existence. In connection with this subject it is well to make it known that the cultivation of sugar-cane, as carried on in our colonies, necessitates a kind of labour which must be always difficult to obtain at low wages in any place where labour is really free. This is a well-known fact, but it is one which people discoursing about black labourers carefully keep out of sight. Do we not see the same thing even in free Australia ? All over that vast island-continent every form of labour and work is done, and well done, and no one complains of the inefficiency of labour. Where labour is scarce, people wanting it have to wait until the free emigrant chooses to arrive and give it. But with the sugar-cane cultivation in Australia this free fabric falls into the dust at once. Here we have the clamour for gangs of coolies, for Polynesian "immigration," for anything to stock the estates with indentured labourers who, once engaged, must work out their term of years, slaves in all but name.

The island of Trinidad has been always noted for the wages given being higher than in any other West Indian island. Next to the Panama Canal and Venezuela it attracts the most emigrant labour from the other islands. These emigrants do not always return to their own islands. With the money they save they buy land and settle in Trinidad as peasant proprietors. This class is becoming a numerous and influential body in the island. Sir T. Graham Briggs, in a letter dated 13th March, 1883, said :—

"The wages for one task in Trinidad is 1s. 8d. The natives only do one task a day, but labourers who go there to make money constantly do two tasks for 3s. 4d., which is, by the way, a proof that the negro will work with sufficient inducements, and also proves the necessity of giving cheap food to our people in the small islands if we are to keep them. A black man in Barbados told me that 1s. 8d. did not go so far in Trinidad as 1s. in Barbados, owing to dear food, but that most of the Barbadians who went there did two tasks, and all could do one and a half."

The Barbadian black man is noted for being the most intelligent labourer in the West Indies. This intelligence, or technical skill, enables him to do more work for a like expenditure of energy than most other black men. The reason why he does not emigrate more readily is because, except at Trinidad, there are no sufficient inducements given him. All the other reasons given are absurd.

The present political organisation of the West Indies is adverse to labour, just as it is adverse to capital and enterprise. Every practical man must admit this. Were they all one colony, labour would get distributed more freely among the parts. Rate of wages depends on character and capacity, but there must be a market. The present system tends to isolate the demand from the supply. The wages a workman wants, *at its lowest,* means that which he must lay out in order to continue able to work. This means subsistence for himself and family. The West Indian black labourer has a small advantage over the European labourer ; there is a limit to lowness in wages. Where wages descend to a point that only the barest existence can be provided out of them, nature comes to his aid ; he can flee to the mountain and forest and demand from nature the bare subsistence of the animal. In the history of the wages of labour one fact stands out conspicuous ; low wages mean low wants, and a decrease in wants means degeneracy. Anything under fair wages cannot lead to prosperity among a people black or white. Labour, on the whole, is underpaid in the West Indies.

Mr. Froude says a vote never did a man any good. It is

certainly not easy to see what good it can possibly be to an individual man.   But the eminent German economist Roscher says :   " High wages follow parliamentary right of suffrage not as phenomena, but as consequences closely related."   There is nothing in the West Indian labour problem to indicate that higher wages would follow on a suffrage, but neither is there anything to show in a contrary sense.   But there is everything almost to show that a cheaper and more effective general government by confederation, combined with an effective and adequate local self-government for the several parts, would lead to better management all round, to a better adjustment of the parts to the whole, to a better system of education, and, finally, to those movements of confidence, capital, and enterprise which precede, if they do not accompany, every onward and upward step of a people.

CHAPTER VIII.

IT will be admitted there is nothing to prove that when a popular form of government replaces an aristocratic form, it always and immediately leads to a better system of taxation or to a better administration of the public funds. This is due to the self-evident fact that incidences of taxation and expenditure affect not only the general welfare of a country, but every individual and particular interest in it. If a bad form of taxation and a corrupt expenditure be adverse to a country's lasting prosperity, it must be adverse to any party in that country. The best policy, therefore, to be pursued by a party, to whichever side it may belong, which has the possession of power in a state, and which desires to continue in that possession with the least molestation and opposition, is to establish and continue a fair and honest system for raising and administering the public revenue. If this almost self-evident truth had been always adhered to by oligarchies and aristocratic forms of government, and by democracies, there would have been fewer changes and fewer movements in an opposite direction. However, in all forms of society, sooner or later, the personal interests of the moment, of the individual, of the family, and of the class, are allowed to dominate over the general interests, and then the day of reckoning is not far off.

The greatest destroyer of the old autocratic and even of close aristocratic systems of government is modern finance. In the days when these were practically the only forms of government known, rulers did not always have to take into account the opinions or sentiments of their people. But in these days no rulers or governments can hope to do much without they obtain public credit and a favourable hearing not only among their own people but among foreigners. To obtain this they are forced to adjust their rule and system of administration after a manner to satisfy the general notion of what is practically best.   If they cannot do this they find it difficult to get money, or have to pay more for it.   The highest quotations for public securities are among those of states with popular forms of government, or those in which the interests of all classes of the people are distinctly and evidently represented by the administration.   This is the more curious because there is nothing to show these latter to be more stable as permanent powers in the world than the other.   Those governments whose people have permitted them to descend to public swindling need not be taken into account.   The public is easily enough swindled even by known professional sharpers.   When a people who ought to have an honoured name descend to this kind of thing, no greater proof can be afforded of their incapacity.   They are obviously wanting in those essential qualities without which neither states nor individuals can hope to gain respect.   They are the losers in the race.

The financial administration of the several West Indian colonies has always been honourable as far as England is responsible for it, and, taken as a whole, there is little or nothing to be said against the honourability of the several local governments on this point.   But honourability does not exclude foolishness and want of understanding and of foresight, and it is to be feared that a good measure of the latter may be discerned both in the methods of raising revenue and in the incidences of expenditure, not in any one of the fifteen colonies only, but in the whole of them.

The government of the West Indies is a costly one.   The worst of it is that every attempt to reduce the cost has tended unmistakably to bring about greater inefficiency.   This is inevitable from the vice of the system.   A small community may very well provide for all the necessities of its local self-government, and may give its proportional payment, according to its wealth and standing, to uphold an effective general government.   But to expect a single small West Indian island to be able to support a general government of its own—as a general government of a progressive British colony should be—is asking too much.   The attempt to do this has failed utterly, and any attempts to prolong the system must cause these colonies to remain in a relatively inferior position.

Attempts have recently been made in a small way to lessen the evils of the system by causing a greater uniformity in methods of taxation in the several colonies, especially with reference to duties of customs. This is only a proof, if proof were wanted, of the desirability of a completer union for all common purposes.

The public expenditure of the fifteen colonies amounts to over £2,062,500 a year. This may not appear excessive for a population of about 1,560,000, but other considerations, besides mere numbering of heads, have to be taken into account when dealing with statistics on the subject of taxation. The yearly annual export of West Indian produce varies; in 1887 it was about £7,600,000 in value. If a similar figure be allowed for the produce raised and consumed by the people, it will be a large allowance. This will make the annual product equal £15,200,000. But as the value of exports in 1887 was very low—in previous years it averaged over £9,000,000—that figure may be taken as an average for a series of years. This will make the average annual product £18,000,000. Taxation, therefore, equals somewhat over 11 per cent. of the yearly product. If now, for comparison's sake only, we turn to the United States, we find the following figures, taken from Henry C. Adams' work, published by Appleton, New York, 1887 (" Public Debts, an Essay on the Science of Finance "):— The total annual product of the United States is estimated at $10,000,000,000, and the total Federal, State, and local expenditure at $800,000,000, or 8 per cent. The rich, prosperous, and well-to-do American people pay 8 per cent. against 11 per cent. paid by the poor backward West Indian people. The position thus stated would be unsatisfactory enough; but, going behind the scenes, we see worse, very much worse. Taxation in the West Indies is so adjusted that it falls chiefly on the people as consumers. Those who make the most profit from the land and the numerous and wealthy absentee owners of large properties practically pay no taxes at all in some islands. How much of the exported produce is owned by these latter cannot be accurately ascertained, but if it be put at £3,000,000 it will be much under what they themselves claim it to be. This will make the proportion of taxation to the annual product *of the taxpayers* as £2,062,500 is to £15,000,000, *or about* 13¾ *per cent. paid by the British West Indian people against 8 per cent. paid by the people of the United States.*

No one would object even to this state of things, viewed from a point of expenditure only, if the incidences of taxation were fair for all, and money's worth was had for it. Poor people must always pay more in proportion for everything than rich people ; this has always been the case, and will probably always continue to be so. But the conditions of the taxation are unjust, the system of taxation is unsound, and the exemptions are unfair to the people of the islands. The little the people really get for this relatively heavy outlay is a startling proof of the unsoundness of the whole system. No people of average common sense, who had a hand in the management of their own affairs, would permit such an unjust and unbusinesslike condition of things to remain on foot a year longer. With this comparatively enormous expenditure the West Indies are noted, on the whole, for having bad roads, bad harbour accommodation, bad sanitary arrangements, bad water supply, poor tumble-down public buildings, insufficient educational appliances, and, in fact, for being burthened with a condition of things so extremely unsatisfactory that, except he has reasonable hopes of a change for the better, no man could fairly recommend a would-be colonist to seek his fortunes there *as a resident.*

The value of the produce raised on estates owned by absentee owners and companies is probably often nearer £5,000,000 than £3,000,000, but they have to pay for raising it. No one objects to absentee owners and companies having land and cultivating it, on condition they enjoy no monopolies over resident owners, and are not permitted to introduce foreign contract labour for their special benefit, and especially on condition they pay a due proportion of the public taxes of the colony. At present they practically pay nothing in some colonies ; and they do not pay their fair share of taxation in any single colony.

Speaking of the West Indian blacks, Mr. Froude says on page 50 : " They have food for the picking up. Clothes they need not." That has been said before Mr. Froude thought of it, and it will probably continue to be repeated. It is an astonishing fact that, notwithstanding our greater, our almost exhaustive, knowledge of tropical countries, most people, even those who visit and cursorily view them, adhere to the old fairy-tale-like notion that men can live on the natural products of the forest in such lands. Men can partially subsist by the chase where game is plentiful, also by fishing, but the earth never yields any fruit anywhere without labour. " In the sweat of thy face shalt thou eat bread." We know how travellers fare in the most magnificent tropical lands in the world when they run short of supplies. If Mr. Froude would make us believe it is easier to raise food supplies for the sustenance of man on a West Indian island than it is in the Isle of Wight, he is equally at fault. An acre of average land in the Isle of Wight will produce more of such food for less labour than a similar acre in Jamaica.

Mr. Froude and his friends dislike " undigested " statistics ; if their stomachs be too weak for such commonplace food as statistics, they must not deal with questions of taxation and should avoid making rash statements like the above. In the year 1886 there was a considerable stir in Jamaica due to some discoveries made by Mr. Haliburton. This gentleman had been residing for over eighteen months in the rural districts of the island, among the black and brown people, and he found a great deal of poverty among them. This was perhaps already known or guessed at, but Mr. Haliburton also found, what was apparently not generally known, that the poor were utterly neglected, and the sick and dying received no medical relief whatever, or so little that it was inappreciable in its effect on the general mass of misery. Mr. Haliburton's latter contentions were contradicted by the authorities, but this gentleman stuck to his guns, and finally it was admitted on all sides that he was in the right, and he was thanked by a grateful press for the public service he rendered the island, in letting it be known that so many of the people were not only poor, but were neglected by the authorities.

During the course of the dispute it was deemed advisable to make an independent public inquiry on the spot. An inquiry of this nature was therefore duly opened at the Letitz district of St. Elizabeth on the 2nd January, 1886. Among the other hitherto unknown facts brought to light was the following :—

"It appears that for six or seven years past the crops have greatly suffered from droughts, and that the people there, though dependent on the produce of their little holdings, have had to subsist for seven months of the year on imported food, which is heavily taxed."

The gentlemen presiding at this enquiry were Mr. Haliburton, Q.C., the Honourable I. Thompson Palache, member of the Legislative Council of Jamaica, Mr. Swaby, J.P., Mr. D. Panton Forbes, a representative on the Parochial Board, Mr. Orth, Inspector of Schools, three Moravian missionaries, and some leading residents. This Lititz district is typical of many others in this island. Even when droughts do not destroy the local food supplies, the quantity raised is not nearly sufficient for the wants of the people. As a matter of fact the small cultivators prefer growing fruit and other articles for the American market, and the Americans in return send their splendid provisions. This is much more satisfactory, and more civilising, than the "picking up" system which Mr. Froude seems to think was the normal one in the West Indies.

It is the same tale in nearly all the islands. Excessive rains, and at wrong periods, can damage and even destroy crops in the West Indies as they do in other countries, as well as droughts and blights. Local famines are common enough. But the greatest proof of all are the returns of imports. The importations of food supplies into the West Indies are proportionately heavier than similar importations into Great Britain from all foreign countries. Nothing could more clearly demonstrate the inaccuracy of Mr. Froude's statement. The importations of food-stuffs from the United States alone into the British West Indies average in value about £1,700,000 a year, or one-fifth of the total imports into these colonies. It must be understood that, for practical purposes, neither corn nor rice is grown in the West Indies. Those who maintain that the people grow, or could grow, their own food supplies, are misleading the public.

The following statement of Mr. Froude's is certainly one of the oddest in his book :—

"The blacks had nothing to complain of, and the wrong at present was on the other side. The taxation falls heavily on the articles consumed by the upper classes. The duty on tea, for instance, was a shilling a pound, and the duties on other luxuries in the same proportion. It did not touch the negroes at all. They were acquiring land, and some thought there ought to be a land tax."

Before commenting on the above, and demonstrating how the statements are opposed to fact, it will be well to give the opinion of the late Sir T. Graham Briggs on the general question. In all the West Indies there was no one more competent to give an opinion on these matters. In a letter dated 4th February, 1882, he says :—

"The Colonial Office has now a great opportunity in these islands (St. Kitts and Nevis), which are Crown colonies, to show its strength, its justice, and its wisdom, by insisting on the food and clothing of the labouring classes being free, and so setting an example to other colonies."

In another letter, dated 28th January, 1883, he says :—

"Without cheap food everything must go to destruction. It is unjust laws (tariffs) which make food dear."

On the 25th November, 1882, he writes as follows, from the island of Nevis, where he had several estates :—

"Although unable to go about much as yet, I have seen many persons, and I have already got very startling information on many points, such as emigration and the terrible destruction of infant life both here and in St. Kitts. In Antigua, of course, it is a notorious scandal and a disgrace to the Government even more than here. I find, too, that several proprietors are alarmed at the emigration and infant mortality, and that they begin to confess that we must have cheap food for our people."

Sir Thomas also sent in a memorandum to the Royal Commissioners while they were in the Leeward Islands, from which the following extracts are taken :—

"The landowner is exempted from taxation ; whereas overseer, clerk, clergyman, their wives and families, are taxed.

"The taxes on food bore heavily on the poor labourers, their wives and children, and bring on scarcity and dearness of food, so that they cannot keep soul and body together.

"With the present price of food an agricultural labourer cannot live and raise his family around him without unremitting exertion, freedom from all sickness, and extraordinary and unusual good fortune. On this point a Barbados labourer told me that in spite of the great advantages he enjoyed in Nevis, of a house and an acre of land free of rent, and constant employment at fair wages, he could not make anything to save, owing to the price of food."

The duty on tea was 1s. a lb. in Jamaica and the Bahamas, but it was comparatively moderate in the other islands   It is not an article extensively used in the West Indies, the people preferring coffee. The duty levied on wheaten flour in the West Indies varies in almost every one of the fifteen colonies, the average being 26 per cent. on first cost at port of shipment; at Jamaica it was 50 per cent. The average duty on corn meal (an article solely consumed by the blacks) averaged 16 per cent. on first cost; but this also varied in almost every colony, some colonies, as Barbados, levying a moderate duty. Rice paid 41 per cent. duty at Jamaica, 27 per cent. at Trinidad, 13 per cent. at British Guiana, and only 6½ per cent. at Barbados. Salt fish paid 18½ per cent., 20 per cent., 30 per cent. duty on first cost, except at Barbados, where it was low, and Trinidad, where it entered free. Salt meat paid 13 to 33 per cent. on its cost, except at Trinidad, where this article was free of duty. Cheese, butter, bacon, hams, sausages, paid 18 to 40 per cent. duty on first cost. Lard, soap, candles, salt, all paid high duties. Refined (loaf) sugar was charged from 25 to 50 per cent. duty on cost. Wines, spirits, and beer paid less in proportion than food. Leaf tobacco (the kind used by the people) paid a duty of from 80 to 140 per cent. on its value; manufactured tobacco paid from 15 to 30 per cent. on its value. The duties on ordinary merchandise and articles used for clothing ranged from the 20 per cent. of St. Lucia and the Bahama Islands to 4 per cent. at Trinidad. The duties on petroleum varied from 8 to 150 per cent. on first cost, according to the colony into which it was imported.

The duties on food, which Mr. Froude says "did not touch the negroes at all," combined with other taxes, simply withdraws from their pockets and scanty earnings the sum of 13s. 7d. per head of population. A man and wife and three children will altogether pay £3 7s. 11d. a year. But this is for bare duties of customs and other forms of taxation only. The importing tradesman, who has to advance duties of customs in cash on perishable food (and in a tropical climate, too), and where money readily commands 10 per cent. interest on sound paper, will want 50 per cent. on his outlay. All this means that a black man's family has to pay a good deal more than the above sum every year to meet one of the most unsound systems of taxation ever devised.

Now, what are the consequences of all this? Starvation. Who knows the misery that lies beneath the surface of every form of society? Those who search. Who by passing along the crowded thoroughfares of London, by visiting the markets and by conversing with the upper classes, would know anything of the real condition of the poor? How long does it take a man to know anything of the actual condition of a peasantry, even when he tries hard to find it out, especially if he be a stranger? Will the mere surface appearance of things tell him anything? The prosperous and well-to-do show themselves; the poor and the miserable hide. This is especially a characteristic of the black man.

The Government medical establishments kept up in the West Indies are, in proportion to taxation and the means of the people, the most costly in the world; but their efforts for good are the least apparent of any in the world. The mass of human misery and disease is too great to be successfully battled against. Mr. Haliburton says :—

"I am quite sure that a majority of deaths among the poor of Jamaica (*i.e.*, among four-fifths of the people) are due, in a large measure, to this cause" (a lack of proper food); "and it becomes a grave question whether the public health would not be better served by increasing and improving the food supply of the people, than by keeping up a costly (medical) system, that only reaches 3 per cent. of the masses in their last illness."

Mr. Craig, a well-known Jamaican, in recently introducing a Poor Law Bill to the local Legislature, showed that out of a population of about 600,000, almost 450,000 might be reckoned as poor, in the sense of needing medical relief. They were poor in the sense of being unable, from time to time, to get enough food, because of the heavy taxes on it. Those that lived by daily labour were bound, sooner or later, after middle age had passed, and the strength and greatest vigour of life had been expended, to fall into disease and misery, and then die in their cabins in the presence of a starving wife and emaciated children. No wonder the British black man prefers to go to Panama and the mines of Venezuela, because he knows if he survives he can return to his island, and buy land of his own, and live poor but independent, as a small peasant cultivator, with somewhat less risk of death from starvation. As a labourer, with the poor wages and dear food, ultimate starvation is certain. The black man is currently accused of not working enough, but where are there men who can labour well and efficiently on an insufficient diet?

"They"—the negroes—"were acquiring land, and some thought that there ought to be a land tax." Just so; no one hought "there ought to be a land tax" while the land was held exclusively by the great owners. But in truth there ought to be a land tax now, and there ought always to have been one. But a just one. The Report of the Royal West Indian Commissioners on the islands they visited, published in 1884, contains much useful information, and one or two valuable suggestions, but their proposed land tax was the most unjust, foolish, and impracticable scheme ever set up. The Colonial Office, it is believed, did not favourably view it; no practical man could. It had the quality of being unsound, and the effect of being mischievous. It alarmed the peasant owners without conciliating the absentee and other great landlords. The interests of the former, *i.e.*, of the people, were openly and distinctly sacrificed to the absentee and other land monopolists. The people will have scant faith in "Royal" or any other Commissions when the results are so incongruous. A "Royal" Commission should be impartial in its report as a judge in his summing-up. When the absence of this impartiality is visible, for reasons unknown, the Report becomes valueless as a guide, and a danger to the unwary.

Above all it is necessary, in legislating for the West Indies, to avoid the appearance of class, or rather race, legislation. What was the proposal of the Commissioners? It was as follows :—A uniform rate of 1s. on every acre or fractional part of an acre of land up to 100 acres, 6d. an acre on every acre beyond the first 100 up to 500 acres, and 1½d. on every acre over 500 acres. The Commissioners found a land tax in Jamaica, but not always in the other islands. The Jamaican land tax was one imposed by the great landowners when they held power, and was as follows :—3d. per acre on all cultivated lands, 1½d. an acre on guinea-grass land, ¾d. on pasture, ¼d. on ruinate or wood. It must be remarked that guinea-grass and pasture lands pay very well, and forests also give profits. Of course with peasant owners all their land is reckoned "cultivated," but the large landowner and the absentee have usually much grass, pasture, and wood. The Commissioners, therefore, quadrupled the tax on *all* the property of the peasant owner, who has never 100 acres. The large landowners may have 100 acres of their estates cultivated on the same terms as the peasant; if more than 100 acres be cultivated they pay only half as much on it as the peasant does, but all their guinea-grass above the 500-acre limit is taxed as before, and the taxes on their pasturages over the 500-acre limit is only doubled. The forest pays more, no doubt, but it costs nothing to keep up, and it increases yearly in value; an occasional small cutting will ease it of all taxes. The big landlord is favoured here openly. The State loses by it. The small resident cultivator is unjustly treated by it. Every element of wrong, of class legislation, and of unsound finance, are accumulated in this proposal. Far-seeing legislators and statesmen in the United States and in Europe are thinking that owners of unoccupied and uncultivated lands should pay a special tax on it, instead of being favoured at the expense of the worker.

It will be of no use to try and tinker up West Indian taxation. The system is unsound in its incidence, unfair and unjust in its application, and disastrous in its consequences. Taxation in these colonies requires to be entirely revised, and to be made business-like and just to all. Above all, imported food must be entirely free from all charges of customs.

CHAPTER IX.

THE FOREIGN WEST INDIES—THE HAYTIAN MYSTERY
EXPLAINED.

ONE may feel it to be one's duty to endeavour to describe the
West Indies as they are, and to enter into the economic
questions which chiefly affect them, but it must become evident
to everyone who does so that the work is onerous. It is
onerous not because of the difficulty to get at necessary facts
and data, which is great, but because the thing is so utterly
unrelieved by any of those circumstances and events which
make so many other studies of people interesting and picturesque. Humanly speaking, there is not and never was anything connected with these regions that can be fairly said to
touch any high chord of sentiment, or arouse any noble or
generous feeling in the human breast, unless it be one of pity
for the slave. The cupidity of the Spaniard, the destruction of
the aboriginal Carib race, the advent of the African slave, the
demoralisation of slave society, the Act of Emancipation, are
each and all useful, economic, and social studies, but they can be
of no special interest to the general public. The struggles for
supremacy between French and English are of more interest,
but they were rather for imperial than local purposes, and they
had little or no effect on the social condition of things in
the islands. In modern times the dreariness of the topic
becomes more marked; we are chained to the planter and
have to hear his grievances. The tale how the few poor inhabitants of Montenegro have successfully maintained their freedom for centuries against the might of the Turkish power is
more interesting than the history of the whole Chinese empire.
A page of Froissart describing the chivalrous times of the Middle
Ages, or one from the stern annals of the sturdy Swiss, arouses

a higher interest than all the doings of all the Great Moguls. Mr. Froude has been able to do that which no one else could do ; he has made it possible for the public to interest themselves in the West Indies. His pages will do that. The public will neither know nor care to know whether many of his statements are inaccurate.

In modern times, at all events, the foreign West Indies possess more picturesque features than our own. Mr. Froude's book shows this clearly enough. Even the study of Hayti would now possess, if the accounts we hear be not all fables, some of the characteristic interest which attaches to central African travel. There is one feature which shows prominently throughout all West Indian concerns, and that is, that although black races differ enormously among themselves, and that these differences are accentuated and localised more or less in the West Indian islands, the African has added to this foundation the distinctive traits of the European races among whom he has chiefly sojourned. Food, cookery, and manners of life have doubtless much to do with this. The French black man, like the white man of Martinique, is more polished and civilised than his fellow-citizen of Guadaloupe, and he acts the Frenchman so completely in his gestures, gait, and manner of life, that, except for physical differences, the resemblance is almost perfect. The Dutch black man has a sturdiness of manner and a sledge-hammer method in giving his views of things, and withal a shrewd common sense, that leave no doubt on the mind which colony he hails from. The Spaniard is equally there in the black man from Cuba ; he has incorporated under his dark skin, slave though he was, some of the salient characteristics, not of the Spanish gentleman, doubtless, but of those other classes so wittily described in " Gil Blas." The British black man, unfortunately, is given to be a wailing and grumbling specimen of humanity like his former master. As is the case with his former master, also, after due allowances are made for temperament, a solid residue of wholesome grievances remain as a kind of stock-in-trade.

All this proves that the African, unlike the picture given of him by Mr. Froude, is open to civilising influences, and is affected by his surroundings the same as any European might be.

In page 280 Mr. Froude makes a statement which reads

funnily—at least if it be intended as a piece of West Indian history :—

> " Looking to the West Indies only, we took possession of those islands when they were of supreme 'importance in our great wrestle with Spain and France. We were fighting then for the liberties of the human race. The Spaniards had destroyed the original Carib and Indian inhabitants."

No one will deny the importance of having had military and naval possession of the West Indian islands in a struggle of the nature referred to by Mr. Froude. It is also quite on the cards that if ever a struggle of a like supreme nature were to recur, the same islands, now thought so slightingly of, would be perhaps of equal value. But, honestly, Britons have really nothing to gain, and can gain nothing, by overstepping the limits of modesty. We were obviously fighting—and rightly fighting—for our own hands. The idea of fighting for the liberties of the human race is a very fine idea, no doubt. It was invented by the French. It has never yet been put into practice by anyone. There are and have been people in the world who fought, and fought successfully, for their own liberties. If any other people aided them they had doubtless very good reasons of their own for doing so. The time may come when people will fight for one another's liberties, as they would for their own, but it has not come yet. Perhaps Mr. Froude does not deem the Africans, we were about that time busily enslaving, part of the human race. The Spaniards did many cruel and abominable deeds in the West Indies ; but neither are our hands clean. We killed off the Caribs in our own islands ; the Spanish and the French did the like in theirs. This is history ; any other way of putting it is mere sensation writing.

Mr. Froude often refers to Hayti. It is the corner-stone of his edifice. He cannot see the British black man having any political rights, however minute, without bringing forward this black republic as a warning. No one would care to defend the acts of the Haytian people or of their government where they go wrong ; and that they have gone very wrong indeed in many directions is obvious. But there is a measure in all condemnations, and Mr. Froude does not keep to that measure which justice in this case demands.

Mr. Froude makes absurdly exaggerated and incorrect

statements respecting Hayti. He talks of Obeah and children killed and salted. He then crosses over to Africa and tells us that all this is done in Africa; that the Haytians over in the West Indies are reverting to cannibalism and all the abominations of their ancestors, and that the British black man will do likewise if we let him. Before demonstrating the complete incorrectness of Mr. Froude's allegations it will be necessary to give some of his own words.

In page 126, speaking of Sir Spencer St. John's work, he says :—

" The republic of Toussaint l'Ouverture, the idol of all believers in the new gospel of liberty, had, after ninety years of independence, become a land where cannibalism could be practised with impunity. The African Obeah, the worship of serpents, and trees and stones, after smouldering in all the West Indies in the form of witchcraft and poisoning, had broken out in Hayti in all its old hideousness, children were sacrificed as in the old days of Moloch, and were devoured with horrid ceremony, salted limbs being preserved and sold for the benefit of those who were unable to attend the full solemnities."

Everyone knows that those Africans who are not Mohammedans or Christians are pagans. But everyone does not know, and Mr. Froude is apparently among these, that very few of the countless pagan tribes of Africa are cannibals, while none of them practise cannibalism in their religious rites. A great number of these pagan tribes practise human sacrifice as well as animal sacrifice, and also offer up food and the fruits of the earth to their divinities. Human sacrifice is offered to the gods, but it is not a very common form of sacrifice. Also when a chief dies his favourite wife or concubines and some slaves are slain and buried with him, because the people believe all these will then continue to sojourn together in the world of spirits. But these forms of pagan belief and burial customs are not by any means universal in Africa. The gods the pagan African desires to propitiate are chiefly malignant and always invisible, except when they elect to show themselves. They have a dwelling-place which may be a grove, or a tree, or a hut, or under a cairn of stones. This invisible god is usually the spirit of some mountain, wood, or river. The god may be male or female; may be deemed black, white, or mulatto, and may be the tutelary deity of a household, a tribe, or a race. Some gods move with the tribes, others are localised. In fact, we see here, clear of all fable and poetic gloss, the belief of the old pagan worlds of Greece and Rome.

The worship Mr. Froude says has been "revived" in Hayti has no counterpart in Africa. The people of the continent do not kill and eat children in their religious rites. The sacrificial offering, when human, is usually a grown person, and the body is not eaten. The African, even as a pagan, is a religious man. His faith is a bad faith, but he acts up to it. The pagan faith of the African teaches him no morality, no sense of right and wrong, and no duties from any Christian standpoint; but it imposes certain personal and tribal obligations, and these he never abandons. When the pagan African turns Mohammedan he becomes a fanatical follower of the prophet; when he becomes a Christian he can fearlessly bear comparison with his white neighbours.

But to return to Hayti. This is what Mr. Froude says of the Haytians on page 183 : "They were equipped when they started on their career of freedom with the Catholic religion, a civilised language, European laws and manners, and the knowledge of various arts and occupations which they had learnt when they were slaves." Lucky Haytians ! Did Mr. Froude when he wrote this not forget what he had been just saying of the black man in the British islands? To take Mr. Froude at his word, the British black men of to-day are not near so well "equipped" as were the Haytians ninety years ago. But the bare fact, which ought to have been thought of long ago when people were endeavouring to account for these proceedings in Hayti, is that the black people of the interior of the island were never Christians; they had never been converted from paganism to Roman Catholicism. A large number of the blacks were pagans at the time of the rising. The most that can be said is that these pagans may have diminished in number during the ninety years that have since elapsed; but the probability that they should have been all converted to a sound Christianity is altogether unlikely, if we take into consideration the political and social state of Hayti during these ninety years. The enormous difficulties thrown in the way of the advance of education and Christianity, by the chaotic condition brought about by successive insurrections and civil strife, would make the subsequent conversion of the whole considerable pagan residue, well known to have existed at the time, entirely improbable.

Prejudice often surpasses jealousy itself in its blindness. The eagerness with which Mr. Froude has seized on the Haytian reports is understandable enough with his frame of mind. But that he should have been so incautious as not to discern the true causes is incomprehensible. He has too low an estimate of the black man to be really of opinion that the Haytian Africans were all Catholics ninety years ago, when only just relieved from the most awful and degrading bondage, as will presently be shown, men were ever subjected to.

In point of fact we have no proofs even now of these Haytian sacrifices upon which to build any solid argument. That sacrifices of some sort have been made, from time to time, appears to be sufficiently established. If they are the sacrifice of live children, which are salted and eaten after death, all that can be said about it is that the Haytian pagans have developed a new and abominable form of pagan rite for which there is no counterpart in Africa itself.

This brings us to another important question : of what African races are these Haytians made up ? There are cannibals in Africa, but few. We know some of them were shipped as slaves. A British cruiser once brought into Sierra Leone a captured slaver. Some of the liberated slaves from this vessel subsequently took to the forest in the neighbourhood and lived as men-eaters, until they were all exterminated. But all the other liberated slaves landed at this port, before and since, became good citizens, excellent Christians, honest tradesmen, and in fact went through all the duties of life in a most praiseworthy manner. The condition of Hayti before emancipation, and much of its condition since, would not tend to civilise a class of men of the above cannibal kind, if they resided in the interior of the island ; and it is from the interior that we hear of these abominable proceedings. That the thing is not common in Hayti, that, in fact, it is almost unknown to the seaside population, is evident. The Haytian local papers referred to it and disputed about it—one editor was imprisoned for maligning the State. That pagan rites in some form or other exist, in which human remains form part, is certain, for people have been tried and even punished by the Haytian courts for taking part in them. Mr. Froude says the authorities have ceased action recently from fear of the people and the necessary exposure. There is really no warrant for this statement. In a disorganised society like Hayti it must be extremely difficult to bring to book any people who do such things, and, indeed, it may be almost better to try other methods, and send priests and ministers to convert and civilise them.

The whole superstructure built up by Mr. Froude on this Haytian myth falls to pieces when the myth itself is shown to be absurd. There can be no relapse where there is nothing to relapse from. To make the picture more effective, Mr. Froude magnifies the Christianity and civilisation of the Haytian slaves of ninety years ago. It is well known a large number of them were far greater savages at that time, due to the vile ill-treatment they received in bondage, than they were when first shipped from Africa. Christianity did great things, no doubt, and improved those few it touched, but it could have had no effect on those it never reached. Sir Spencer St. John's book is misleading in the same way as Mr. Froude's, but it is not deliberately so. Sir Spencer knows nothing of the Africans in Africa, and he apparently thought that those who practised pagan ceremonies in Hayti had been formerly Christians. This is an error, but it is a mild one, because its effects were limited. But Mr. Froude has taken it up, has accepted it, and has widely extended it. It therefore becomes necessary to point out and expose it. The Haytians therefore who do these things have not relapsed into paganism; they simply were never converted to Christianity. The explanation is obvious and reasonable, but it would not have answered Mr. Froude's object to seek for it.

This Haytian question being put on its true footing, it is nevertheless obvious the people have gained nothing by absolute independence. They have gained nothing because they were insufficiently "equipped" for it. The Catholic religion had not reached them *as a religion*. How could it? Only its mere outward formulæ were observed by their masters and mistresses; they themselves, in most cases, were deemed unfitted by their owners to frequent the churches. The priests no doubt did their duty to some extent, and made some show of ministering to the blacks equally with the whites. But the church was essentially the church of the whites. There were priests who thought differently; but the slave-owners could not bring themselves to that opinion. Christianity also interfered with the owners' arrangements ; these objected to binding ties between men and women and between children and parents, and Christian ceremonies would make them binding—even legally binding—in those days. There was a varnish of Christianity along the coast and in the towns and villages, but the paganism of the blacks in the interior and more remote places remained practically untouched.

The large estate owners lived in France and sent agents to supervise their properties in Hayti. They were insatiable in their demands for produce and money to keep up the expensive style of living they followed in Paris. The poor slaves were worked to death, ill-fed, and cruelly maltreated. It is notorious that the conduct of the French towards their slaves in Hayti surpassed in hardness, brutality, and vileness, anything known in the English or Spanish islands ; and yet Mr. Froude says, page 258 : "The French planters had done nothing particularly cruel to deserve their animosity." They only did all that men could do, by oppression, cruelty, and wrong, to lay the seeds that must sooner or later bear fruit in a terrible uprising of the oppressed, or a servile war waged to the death. It came, as comes the hurricane, the typhoon, or the tornado. The breath of the French Revolution stirred to its depths the corrupt and rotten mass, and the whole fabric was swept away and borne down in ruin and bloodshed.

Over the ruins was set up what we see to-day, and certainly the sight is not a pleasant one. The Christian religion has no solid footing in Hayti, and can we expect civilisation without it ? The ninety years that have elapsed have been chiefly spent in internecine insurrections. The richer people now send their sons to Paris ; and these return to their island with a showy education that, too often, mocks at religion and apes Voltairianism. The state of things is bad. The one remedy is missionary exertion, and the spread of education *with it.* Who is to do this, or how it may be done, are questions that cannot be touched on here. But Hayti is not altogether without some good points either. It has had able and wise men in the past, and it has them now ; men who did, and are doing, their utmost to place their country on a higher level. The actual president, General Salomon, is a very able man indeed, and the energy he shows, if somewhat arbitrary in appearance in our eyes, finds strong support in the island both amongst the most enlightened and the majority of the people.

And Mr. Froude thinks an English colony must necessarily follow this career of Hayti, if the people be granted some reasonable measure of local self-government under British guidance? It is in page 124 that Mr. Froude says : " Exceptions are supposed proverbially to prove nothing, or to prove the opposite of what they appear to prove. When a particular phenomenon occurs rarely, the probabilities are strong against the recurrence of it." He would not say this of the Haytian " ceremony," although a sound reason can be given for it, and the " particular phenomenon " has never occurred anywhere else yet. But when a black man shows capacity for good, it is immediately seized hold of ; the " particular phenomenon " must then not be deemed to show that many black men can equally rise, whereas as a matter of fact that hundreds, nay thousands, have done so.

The condition of things in Cuba struck Mr. Froude, but it is not wonderful that he should have misunderstood the causes. It is simply impossible for Mr. Froude to read the black man. He measured him in his own mind long ago by a false measure, and this measure he carried with him to the West Indies, and wherever he meets with the black man he outs with it. After all he had heard about the Spaniards, more especially after all he had written about them, it evidently struck Mr. Froude that the African in Cuba felt himself more of a man than the British black man in our islands ; he was more happy, more laborious, more a part of the place. Mr. Froude can only account for this phenomenon by saying, on page 303, that the hidalgo is himself somewhat of a nigger by blood, and therefore can have no contempt for the " niggers. The high-bred and pure-blooded Norman-Saxon of our islands can pare his nails in public without fearing that the blood of Ham may appear under their delicate rose tints. With the Spaniard it is different; did not the Moors conquer Spain long ago ?

No Spaniard has written, or could have written, of the black man after Mr. Froude's manner. The Spaniard has many faults, but he is no hypocrite. He says he thinks slavery good because he believes it paid him ; he never affected to say it was good for the black man also. Perhaps the Spaniard in some respects was more cruel to his slave than the Englishman, but withal he treated him more as a man. The Englishman, if less cruel, treated his slaves as cattle. When, therefore, the black man becomes free the Spaniard frankly accepts the *fait accompli;* he treats him as a free man without any of Mr. Froude's reserves. The Spaniard never affected to think the African was born to be a slave; but he was quite willing to make him one for his own profit. ⸗ Mr. Froude thinks slavery was good for the black man; but if it must be done away with then the next nearest thing to slavery that can be put in practice is best for him. He says the English whites have a supercilious contempt for "niggers" always. We here see the true cause for much that is otherwise inexplicable. The British black man has a liking for and confidence in the British government, but he has no special regard for the individual Englishman; this means that he believes in justice. The Spanish black man dislikes (or did so until recently) his government, but has much regard, sometimes even personal affection, for the individual Spaniard ; this means that he has self-respect. He regards the Frenchman much as he does the Englishman. The Portuguese he has no regard for at all. The Spanish gentleman does not think it necessary to hedge himself around by a supercilious demeanour from anyone; and the negro therefore treats him with that familiar respect which is the surest sign of good breeding both in master and man. There are ways and manners of life and conduct that are difficult to define, and explain, but which have more effect on the real courtesies of life than the more obvious and accepted forms of outward demeanour. In the days of slavery a Spaniard would perhaps work his slave to death more readily than an English-man, but he would let the priest minister to the dying moments of his slave as if he were one of his own household.

The population of the islands of Cuba and Porto Rica is about 2,200,000, of whom half are whites, and they are steadily increasing There is a large militia force, comprising horse, artillery, and foot, and a considerable marine force, which would be found very serviceable in case of invasion. The Cubans would like to be under the stars and stripes flag, but they would resist to a man being placed under any other. Over ninety per cent. of the sugar raised goes to the United States, as well as two-thirds of the bale tobacco and two-fifths of the cigars. Great Britain sends about £2,000,000 a year in merchandise.

Much can be said against Spanish rule, but the Government of Spain never handed over her islands to a monopoly of merchants, to be worked for their sole profit, as was done by Downing Street with our British islands. The British merchants who have ruled in these islands so long have ever looked upon them as mere workshops out of which the most money was to be got at the minimum of cost. Hardly a white man ever went there except as a government official, or as clerk or overseer for one of these merchants or merchant planters. The resident whites of other days were made bankrupt by a special law, or left because there was no more room for them. A more degrading system of rule for a colony was never yet put into practice. We are now astonished at the result, and at the difference observable between Jamaica and Cuba. A true cause for wonder is that things are not worse. Were it not for the deep corruption of the Administration, with which the people have nothing to do, Cuba would be a very prosperous place.

The Danish island of St. Thomas, so well known as a free port and a port of call, has lost much of its old importance. It is one of the Virgin group of which England is the chief owner, but of which she makes no use. It takes about £225,000 a year of British merchandise.

The Dutch islands are very small and unimportant, but the most, perhaps, is made of them. The Dutch colony of Surinam, on the mainland, is in an entirely stationary condition. There is nothing in its government or in its surroundings to attract capital or colonists; there are too many countries possessing greater attractions in Central America. Surinam, however, shows strong indications of being rich in gold deposits, and if these ever come to be properly discovered they may do something for the place on condition things be fairly managed. The Dutch system of dealing with subject races has been much praised by British lovers of bureaucratic rule. The Dutch themselves are beginning to find it to be disastrous. The fact is that no man, however low he may be in mental condition when laid hold of, can be made into a mere producing machine without evil results following sharp behind. The order of nature is God's order, and those who attempt to run counter to it pay in the end the bitter price. The Dutch power was a real power once ; when its chief enemies were tyrants, bigots, and oppressors. Since it has used its dominion for mere lucre it has fallen so low that it now only lives on in sufferance. Will all the fortunes made out of manipulated natives pay for this inglorious fall ?

The French West Indies suffer somewhat like our own. The rule of France differs in details from British rule, but the principle is identical ; the islands are regarded by home French-men as tropical plantations or gardens, of which money is to be made, rather than colonies of men. Nevertheless, the French, on the whole, give a better system of local self-government. The system of local administration established in France is extended to certain of her colonies, and among these are ranked Martinique and Guadaloupe. But although the system is extended, it is not so in its entirety; there are restrictions which cut down this liberty to somewhat minuter dimensions. Our trade with the French West Indies is small ; they only take about £170,000 a year of our goods. The French black men are loyal to France in recent times. Martinique and Guada-loupe send representatives to the Paris Chamber of Deputies and to the Senate. They have sent black men, and men certainly not white. What would Mr. Froude say to this ? The French colony of Cayenne on the mainland is in a lower category than the islands. Under the present system it is certain never to be much more than a mere name on the map.

San Domingo is chiefly known for having succeeded in raising a loan on which it never pays the interest. The place has great natural advantages ; beyond this it has nothing what-ever to recommend it.

The great rivals of the future with regard to all the West Indies will be the Central American States. The population of this region, including Venezuela and the Columbian States to Guatemala, is reckoned at about 8,000,000. The neigh-bouring Mexican provinces of Yucatan and Campeachy have about 320,000 inhabitants only. Most of the people of the above countries are aboriginal in race, but numerous white men of almost every nationality have carried there an astonishing amount of capital. The West Indian African is the most prized as a labourer in the open, and he can earn the most wages of any man. There are believed to be 7,000 British black men engaged at the gold mines of the Orinoco. The British imports into these Central American regions may be valued at not under £3,000,000.

The Foreign West Indies will always be of some importance to their British neighbours, but they will never be of that value which they ought to be for trade and intercourse while our present system lasts. The British West Indies are being now overshadowed by Cuba and the Central American States. To recover the relative position they ought to hold in the Caribbean Sea they must be all confederated into one colony.

CHAPTER X.

RELIGION in the West Indies, as is the case everywhere else in the world, is, and will be, the measure of the true civilisation of the people. It is the measure of true civilisation everywhere, even when it does not appear to be so. The decline of religion among a people is inevitably and closely followed by a decay of their civilisation, as surely as the rise of this civilisation was due to the religion they now contemn. Of course the character of the civilisation depends on the form of the religion and on the nature of its teaching. In dealing with the West Indian people, however, we have this point settled for us ; the only religion for all practical purposes known there is the Christian.

The moral grandeur of the Christian religion as a teacher is due to the fact that it develops the intellectual powers of the people who follow its teaching closely and truly. All sciences, all civilising arts, even worldly well-being and political stability, necessarily follow this development, and increase with its increase. Why ? Because Christianity teaches and imposes independence of character and self-reliance ; it insists on personal responsibility and on individuality of judgment, and now it insists on education also. The whole argument is included in these facts ; it is therefore the civiliser.

Mr. Froude says that Protestantism, as a positive creed, shows a marked decay, and that it may be advisable for the Protestant powers of Europe to patch up a kind of reconciliation with the old spiritual organisation that was shattered in the sixteenth century by the Reformation. He then, on the same page, 234, makes the following remark :—

"A religion, at any rate, which will keep the West Indian blacks from falling back into devil-worship is still to seek. .... In spite of the priests, child murder and cannibalism have reappeared in Hayti ; but without them things might have been worse than they are, and the preservation of white authority and influence in any form at all may be better than none."

That Protestantism or any other form of Christianity as a positive creed is decaying out of the world is contested by authorities quite as competent as Mr. Froude is to give an opinion on this weighty matter. But there is one phase of Christianity that is always decaying and always being patched up afresh—namely, the State Churches. These have always been the bane of Christianity. Wherever and whenever the ministers of the gospel ceased to be ministers and followers of Christ only, by becoming likewise the servants of states and princes, they have lost the influence they should have possessed among the people. In France, religion—the State religion—became so corrupt, and so allied its own corruption to the deeper political corruption of the times, that the inevitable fall of the one led to the fall of both. The Church in France has not yet recovered from this fall. Wherever Christianity has a firm Biblical hold of the masses of the people, and thus permeates them, the upper social strata, including the state itself, may become as irreligious as it pleases ; it will not affect the multitude or destroy the stability of things. If the religion becomes corrupt, as religions are apt to, the reformer always and inevitably comes forth from among the people whose general convictions he embodies. In England the religion and the civilisation of the people were thus twice saved in recent times : once by the Puritans, and once by the rise of dissent. On each occasion the State Church was rudely shaken and warned ; but it took the warning and strengthened itself, not by seeking alliances with other State Churches, but by labouring to get at the hearts of the people. It is quite possible reforms may be needed in many churches in Europe. With Mr. Froude the mere fact of an old institution requiring the reforms demanded by the age is in itself enough to condemn it altogether. Reform in any shape is a thing so bad that the mere fact of an institution being reformed renders it valueless. He regrets that his days should have to be passed in these degenerate times, and in pages 305-6 gives his opinion that the Reformation of the sixteenth century has, on the whole, been mischievous, and that Charles V, and Philip II, were right after all,

Mr. Froude does not believe in the efficacy of the religion of Christ to keep the West Indian black man from the worst forms of idolatry, or even from child-murder and cannibalism. It has been already shown in previous chapters that child-murder and cannibalism are not known to be practised in Africa itself as part of the religious ceremonies in pagan rites. It has also been shown that the Haytians referred to have not fallen back into paganism from Christianity, for the sufficient reason that they were never converted to Christianity. Besides, some of us will require further proofs of these statements about Hayti—with more precision as to facts—before accepting the whole bald statement. We shall want to know whether the children were really murdered ; in fact the usual judicial proofs demanded in such cases must be forthcoming before rendering judgment. We all know that poor ignorant pagans are capable of doing things that horrify, but as we know of no such doings in Africa itself, or anywhere else in the West Indies, as are alleged to take place in Hayti, the statement that they occur in a wild district, of that island demands more precise confirmation than we have yet been provided with. Similar accusations have been made against Jews and others in Europe, even recently, and were believed in by large bodies of people, notwithstanding their gross improbability.

But, assuming that all this information is got at, and the whole case is proved against Hayti, what has that to do with the question ? The pagan African was captured and was taken to Hayti a century ago ; he was there brutally ill-treated ; he was liberated from bondage by a bloody insurrection ; he was yet a pagan, but a pagan without the restraints of family or tribe as in Africa ; he had therefore fewer chances of improvement than he would have had in Africa itself. If this pagan develops a new form of devil-worship in Hayti, it will only be one more indictment added to the weighty load the slave-exporters and slave-dealers have already to bear. But all this is beating the air. It has besides really nothing to do with the British black man with whom we are dealing. This Haytian mystery may be an interesting psychological and social study, and it is to be hoped the government of the island—if such a chaos may be so called —will some day aid the experts in studying the phenomenon; but it is entirely beside the main question.

Mr. Froude is on the search for a religion of sufficient

efficacy to overcome the phantoms born of his own too exuberant imagination. He need not search far. If he rejects Christianity, he can find safety in Mohammedanism. This faith is firmly established in Africa among countless negro tribes, and they are all as free from paganism as may be desired —as free from it as the worshippers in Westminster Abbey itself. They will not kill children for the purpose of eating them. They would even look upon as dirt beneath their feet Christians who would defile their bodies by eating sucking pig or ham.

But before saying Christianity can do nothing, why not try and do something with it? The State Church of England did almost nothing in the West Indies for 200 years, and it did nothing in Africa ever, until quite recent times. How could it do anything worthy the name of Christianity? It never affected to teach the people in the sense of raising them. Its ministers did not go to the slave as a minister of Christ, but rather as an official of a social order of things of which he was paid to be an upholder, and in which the slave was—what Mr. Froude tells us he was. But, in truth, Mr. Froude says all this himself, and says it forcibly in page 232 : " I could not find that the Church of England in Jamaica either was at present or ever had been more than the Church of the English in Jamaica." Just so ; and what this church was in Jamaica, it was everywhere else in the West Indies.

Mr. Froude is no lover of dissent because he is no lover of freedom. The great religious movements and revivals brought about by the Puritans and Dissenters not only saved Christianity and civilisation in these realms ; they also saved the liberties of the people of England. If he cared to see what was going on in the West Indies, Mr. Froude might have noted the very different action of the dissenting bodies as missionaries compared to his State Church.

The Church of England failed to do anything worth recording in the West Indies, but the great dissenting bodies have taken the people in hand and they are making them Christians. Mr. Froude only interviewed two Moravian missionaries during his trip, among the hundreds of ministers of dissent that were at work everywhere. The Moravians were modest and did not magnify the virtues of their congregation. They were not enthusiastic about their black sheep, Mr. Froude says ; but a

Moravian minister tells him (page 250) that his poor black sheep, if not better than the average English labourer, are no worse. They were called idle, but they would work for fair wages regularly paid. In other words, the Moravians deem the Jamaican black labourers as good as English labourers. The way Mr. Froude puts all this, and the conclusions he draws, makes one curious to know what are his views, at bottom, about the English labourer himself. The dissenting sects of Christianity are now all-powerful in the West Indies and overshadow the State Church completely. The vast majority of the people are being collected within the folds of these bodies. We see one consequence of this in the disestablishment of the State Churches by the Colonial Office in some of the islands and their projected disestablishment in the remainder The chief dissenting bodies are the Methodists and the Baptists, but there are several others. All these bodies are doing, and effectively doing, the work the State Churches neglected to do. The black man prefers being a dissenter to being a State Churchman, notwithstanding the social dignity supposed to be attached to the latter. He sees and he feels that he is regarded in the latter, at least by his fellow white-worshippers, more as a pariah than anything else. The intensely respectable, prim, unsympathetic affair, called church-going, described by Mr. Froude on pages 237-8, reminds one of the mere formality of a church-parade. If ever there was any life in such a thing it has clearly died out. It is as dead as the slavery it rather upheld than contended against. It was always the church of the whites and not of the Gospel. The black man is received by the great dissenting bodies with the right hand of fellowship. He is deemed equal. He is given the Bible, and he is taught it thoroughly. He is therefore becoming a Christian not in outward form only but in reality—a Christian of the sound English type that has made England what she is.

The Roman Catholic Church in the West Indies is a power in some of the islands, but it has also in these places been the church of the whole people. The Catholic Church has not always allied itself with the particular state within whose civil jurisdiction it has its ministers, and in these cases it possesses most real power among the multitude. The priests and bishops of this church have been sometimes paid by the State (from the people's taxes) the same as the Protestants, but it has never been the State Church in the West Indies. It has sometimes been made a subject of controversy which form of Christianity is best adapted for the black man. Mr. Froude says the priests have failed in Hayti. That they have not made the Haytians into good Christians is self-evident enough. On the other hand people cannot rightly be said to have failed in doing a thing which they have never yet tried to do. The conversion of the Haytians has never yet been effected, and has scarcely been attempted, for want of the right men, or for lack of means, or for want of opportunity. The Catholic Church does not pretend to have reached the bulk of the Haytian people; the priests say they have not had sufficient men or means to do so. In our own islands a somewhat similar complaint has been heard. As a matter of fact the evangelisation of the British colonies would to-day be terribly backward had it depended on the British Government; if not so badly backward as in Hayti, still discreditably so. The noble independent Christian associations of Great Britain have filled the void. These bodies Mr. Froude does not refer to. What would Great Britain itself be to-day without them ?

But neither does it ever answer to expect too much. A moderate and gradual upward movement is all that can be looked forward to. We must not expect more from the negroes than we see accomplished in Europe. Only fifty years ago they were slaves and treated as cattle. They are uneducated ; they are poor ; they are heavily taxed. Expensive administrative establishments are kept on foot out of their taxes, while the provision made for educating them is totally inadequate. England had a manifest duty to accomplish in these colonies, and she never even tried to do it. The planters did nothing for education, for religion, or for civilisation. They do nothing now. All the popular schools, almost, are paid for chiefly, if not entirely, by the contributions of the black population. These poor people are not yet in a position to give enough to ensure competent teachers. But, notwithstanding all these drawbacks, let us see what they have done in little more than a single generation of freedom. We shall then be in a better position to show that Mr. Froude has traduced the character of the British black man most unwarrantably.

In Jamaica all the teachers are coloured men and women. Their average wages come to 12s. 9d. a week each ; the same as a porter or gate-keeper at a local public office. That most of them are incompetent is only what we must expect. The school attendances average 11 per cent. of the whole population of the island; 232,000 are able to read, or read and write, out of a total of 600,000 souls. But in 1881 only 22,000 adult negroes could write in Jamaica. The coloured parents take much interest in the periodical examinations. In those which may be termed the Protestant islands, the school attendances were highest; Jamaica, Antigua, St. Kitts, Nevis reaching 11 per cent., and Barbados 20 per cent., in the Catholic island of Trinidad 7 per cent., and St. Lucia $6\frac{1}{4}$ per cent. only. All the colonies vary from one another. There are just complaints of want of schools in suitable localities, and of children being over-employed on estates. The labour of these children, of course, is cheap. There is much, very much, to be done; but every indication points to the encouraging fact that all which remains to be done for education can be done, and will be done, if only the local governments be empowered to do it.

In the fifteen British colonies there are church and chapel sittings at present provided for one in four of the whole population. This, of course, is not government doing. Of registered Christian churches and chapels there are about 1,100. Unlike many places in the world most of these sittings are occupied at service-time. The British black men and black women and their children are all great chapel-goers, especially in those islands where the dissenters are strongest. Mr. Froude neither saw nor heard aught of this really considerable upward movement in religion and in education; of course he did not. His informants perhaps knew little of it themselves.

Speaking of the morality of a people is always difficult; the surface estimate is usually a false one: nothing demands a deeper and more searching study. Mr. Froude did not attempt to study it; but it has been seen in Chapter V. he has pronounced a deliberate opinion against the blacks nevertheless. He was evidently sometimes puzzled, however. This is what he says, speaking of some black women, page 154:—

"I can only say that if their habits were as loose as white people say they are, I did not see a single licentious expression either in face or manner. They seemed to me light-hearted, merry, innocent, young women, as free from any thought of evil as the peasant girls in Brittany."

He immediately afterwards describes a scene he was witness of; it was a dispute between a black woman and a mulatto woman, in which the former upheld that mulattoes were creatures of human wickedness, and she had the best of the argument, the audience being with her. Now, the above quotation and anecdote are remarkable; rightly estimated and balanced, they say much for the black people whose morality Mr. Froude has elsewhere so decried. His white informants tell him that all black women are immoral, but he admits appearances are against the assumption. He is afterwards witness of a scene which points the moral. The black woman knows well enough that all communications between white men and the women of her race are usually immoral, and she therefore energetically protests against it. Mr. Froude somewhat misses the point in recounting this anecdote.

The question of illegitimacy is another and really separate question. Those who know the blacks best admit they have not the characteristics which usually accompany licentious acts. Illegitimacy is with them a defect, no doubt, but it is due more to economic causes than to moral depravity. Lecky, in his history of European morals, warns us how the social condition of a people must be well known and understood before a charge of unusual immorality can be safely brought against them. The difficulties of complying with legal formalities, the customary expenses of popular usage, low wages, may each and all hinder marriage and lead to a condition of society to be reprehended and deplored; but it would be absurd to draw conclusions not warranted by the premises. By habitual custom marriages among blacks, when church service is a part of the ceremony, is an expensive affair which carries off perhaps six months wages or more. But when Mr. Froude says they are married but not *parsoned*, he forgets that a marriage before a registrar is binding in law. The blacks, however, seem not to take much to the latter; they wait for prosperous times. In the Roman Catholic islands (where the French laws in these matters are in force), a marriage legitimates the children already born, and even a death-bed marriage for the purpose is not uncommon. In the islands where British law only prevails this method does not avail, and the child born before (what in this instance may fairly be called " official") wedlock are illegitimate for ever. With the black people, as a general rule, the unions are permanent. There are exceptions of course ; men go away to other islands seeking work, or go to the gold mines of the Orinoco or to Panama and never return. Instances of a similar kind are not unknown in Great Britain. In some European Christian countries the figures of illegitimacy have reached the West Indian level, but without the same causes or excuses for it.

There is nothing to be gained by placing the British black man on a higher level than he is entitled to, but neither can any good be done by lowering him below his merits. All that he can demand is justice. This the British people will give him. And they will not expect too much from a man who was torn from his home and severed from every natural human tie by slave-dealers, and was taught to behave himself rather as an animal than as a man, until his emancipation only fifty years ago. In order that he may raise and perfect himself they will place in the hands of the colonists—white and black —the means of raising their islands by their own local efforts to the standard of civilisation demanded by the age.

" Where the Spirit of the Lord is there is liberty."

CHAPTER XI.

LOCAL SELF-GOVERNMENT.

THERE are two Britains—the Smaller and the Greater. The designations have been accepted into the language ever since a distinguished statesman invented them to denote the home Britain and the Britain beyond the seas.

The Britain beyond the seas, or Greater Britain, however, requires to be itself subdivided, because it contains within its folds two kinds of countries so entirely distinct from one another that it is impossible to even imagine anything more different.

There is the greater Britain due to colonisation from home ; made up of real Englands, Scotlands, Wales, and Irelands, with a dash of Continental European elements. The colonies comprising this subdivision develop on the same lines as the parent country, but with more rapid and longer strides, and they surpass it in the value they attach to individual freedom and to the powers of education, intelligence, and industry. They are the homes of freedom to-day ; they are destined in the future to rank among the chief powers of the world.

The other subdivision is made up of tropical dependencies and conquered provinces inhabited by diverse races of men, the great majority of whom have little or nothing in common with the people of the United Kingdom. Freedom here is a minute plant of stunted growth, even when attempted to be introduced, which it rarely is. Here we see at work the forces born of Empire and rough war ; we see despotism in all its shapes, from the rigid to the benign, but true liberty never.

Both these divisions of Greater Britain have influence at home in the shaping of the public opinion of the people, but they are influences of a very different nature : that of the free colonies is for good, and it is happily a growing influence; the dependencies born of Empire have no direct influence of their own in the United Kingdom; but the official, trading, and planting classes, which rule and manage them, have a great deal, and, unhappily, it is not always an influence for good.

It will be seen at once how important it is to maintain a distinction which so deeply divides the two divisions of the Greater Britain beyond the seas—the free Colonies and the bureaucratically ruled dependencies.

The people inhabiting the last-mentioned division may be fairly said to have no influence whatever of their own in the United Kingdom, that is to say, in the realm through which they are governed; but another influence, and a powerful one, is always at work, regulating their fortunes and destinies for them. This influence (in which the inhabitants themselves are never represented) is wielded by a body made up of very mixed materials.

In the eyes of the people of England it is the Ministers of the Crown for the time being, and the permanent high officials in London, and the several governors they delegate, who wield all this influence and power, through Parliament, but they are mistaken.

In the numerous Crown Colonies and conquered dependencies there is a small host of military and civil officials, who, on first joining the service, take with them the usual traditional sentiments of Englishmen; but, in course of time, and unobserved by themselves, these sentiments get replaced by others born of their new environment, and they eventually settle down to hold the traditional opinions of the order into which they are enrolled; these opinions may be best expressed by the words "bureaucratic imperialism."

Another powerful body are the tropical planters, who, although in recent times their power in the colonies has been much curtailed, and their influence over the home administration is less than formerly, have considerable local influence with the governors and officials ruling in these dependencies.

A third body, of much greater weight than the above, are the British merchants and traders: this body has powerful representatives of its several interests in the City of London, at the chief commercial ports, at all the great manufacturing towns, and in Parliament.

Any one who cares to study the matter for himself will find out that these three bodies—that is to say, the civil and military officials, the planters, and the British merchants—have, on the whole, identical views as to how the dependencies should be governed. For them mankind is divided into two distinct sections; those made to rule, and those made to be ruled. The officials, and the British planters and merchants of their way of thinking, deem themselves by birth and hereditary right to belong to the former, and the non-British inhabitants of all the dependencies to the latter. Under these circumstances liberty, as understood at home, has little place in their creed, except it be that which of right must be accorded to their own order and race. Liberty, in any other sense, is a word they utter with a disdain befitting an official of the Great White Tzar.

After a time, with pensions or realised fortunes, numbers of these officials, planters, and merchants, retire to England, and it is rare to meet a man among them who does not support, by all the influence he possesses, the old system of rule—the system of irresponsible bureaucratic rule. Many of these have seats in the Parliament of the United Kingdom.

As in most things human, there are exceptions to the above rule, both in the dependencies and at home. In both places are a few officials, and numerous planters and merchants, who are as liberal in their views as the average Briton, and the counter influence they wield tends somewhat to mitigate the effects of the rigid despotisms in operation. But, on the whole, it must be admitted that the influence of the majority of these official, planting, and trading classes, and their representatives at home, while it tends materially to keep extending the boundaries of the existing empire, tends greatly to retard the proper development of the numerous dependencies. Even the material wealth, by which these classes mostly profit, can be clearly shown to be less than it might, and should, be, because the influence they wield favours monopolies and the various forms of restrictive legislation in many dependencies.

Here in England we have every day brought under our notice that millions of mankind, of every race but our own, are ruled bureaucratically and despotically by Englishmen. The agents of this rule out in the dependencies return to the parent England, and their influence is felt in commerce, in industry in society, and in the cabinets of ministers. As has been said the influence of this section of the Greater Britain is not invariably for good. It is not invariably for good because it is often un-English, and it is un-English because it runs counter to the grain of liberty which traverses the whole history of the English people from the signing of Magna Charta to the latest reform. It is also known to be an influence that reaches far; how could it be otherwise? Of brilliant attainments and great administrative ability and business experience, these men are appealed to by the home public for their special knowledge; and the home public, which knows nothing of the matter or of the people in question, is guided by their views; it is told of the beneficence of a stringent paternal rule; it has also whispered in its ear how these millions of people of other races are backward, or degraded, or weaklings, or are otherwise unfitted to possess any of those elementary rights of freemen Englishmen so dearly prize. These statements are backed up by those thousands of other officials in the dependencies, and by those planters, merchants, and traders, dealing with these dependencies, who deem their interests are best served by the system being continued. Hence it comes about that Englishmen at home begin to think in their hearts that liberty after all may be prejudicial and dangerous to society in their dependencies; therefore, the plant of liberty, so strong of growth at home, never gets its seeds sown in these places. England, liberal England, herself advances daily in freedom, whilst these Imperial dependencies seem destined for years yet to come to remain under stringent bureaucratic rule.

Were it not for these influences, which run counter to the sentiments of the British race and the genius of the British people, the consolidation of the Empire would have been far more advanced than we see it to-day. It would be an interesting study to trace the various steps by which such large and intelligent classes of Englishmen came to have opinions so different from those for which the nation has ever been renowned at home. The cause is obviously due to the fact that these dependencies have never been otherwise ruled by us. Where there are no recent traditions of liberty or of public life the ruling classes quickly fall into a groove out of which extrication becomes difficult. In most cases it would have been difficult, and in some perhaps even dangerous, to have introduced the germs of liberty into these dependencies; consequently, the official, planting, and trading classes, always preferred the *status quo*, and the majority of these, if they had their own way, might continue to prefer it, until the writing on the wall preceded the end.

Those who care more for the permanent consolidation of British power and influence than for the passing interests of any section of the community have long been of opinion that a change is wanted in this matter of administration. Since England first formed or obtained her dependencies the world has much altered; powers are being born and others are growing that did not then exist; the telegraph, steam, education, and travel, have transformed the face of society, and the people are nowhere the same as they were. Had England been more true to herself than she has been this subdivision of the Greater Britain would have been grappled to her with hooks of steel; but she lent her ear too readily to the flatterer; she allowed these dependencies to drift along without making efforts to assimilate them. Had she made these efforts she would have succeeded long ago. These dependencies, instead of being detached satellites, which a war or a difficulty would sever from her without their feeling it, would to-day be integral parts of a mighty whole. It was a very simple thing that England had to do: she had only to set on foot those forms of local self-government which have been so powerful for good everywhere, not only within her own borders but wherever else in the world they have been established.

There are people who look askance and with suspicion upon every local strengthening of a colony, upon every Act of Federation, every drawing together of separate interests, every combination for general purposes and common needs. Divide and govern—the bureaucratic motto—has been the system adopted by the generality of Governments which have had dominions beyond their own precincts; it is a maxim always present in the official spirit, and it can only be kept in check by that larger intelligence which comes from the teachings of experience. Especially is this maxim of Governments deemed sound when people are dealt with who are not of the same race as the rulers. Hence the British people, despite that common sense and capacity for business-like administration which characterises them, are apt to fall astern of the times in their dealings with those parts of the empire where the inhabitants do not happen to have the same racial origin as themselves. Hence, also, the danger, as the Empire grows and otherwise consolidates, of the appearance of a cleavage ever widening and separating the more favoured from the less favoured parts.

An Empire ruled as England rules the majority of her dependencies may continue to hold together by habits of routine, by the aid of fortuitous circumstances, and by the knowledge that force of arms can be always applied in case of contumaciousness, but by no other means. We know how this kind of thing always ends. In the days of danger, which come to all, England will find the millions, that would have willingly borne arms to support an Empire in which they had some valuable rights, will desert, perhaps even turn against, her, because they have nothing to gain by doing otherwise.

The actual system can have only two possible results. One is that in every state which contains within its folds other races of men besides the British, the latter must for ever dominate over and hold in subjection all the others ; but this is a phase in the world's history from which we all hope we are emerging—the history of wars, suppressed risings, and dominations. It is a vain mockery, also, to tell the people held in subjection in these dependencies, as we are apt to tell them, that the Imperial Government knows of no distinctions of race ; that all are equally treated, because all are equally without citizen rights and liberties. This may be so ; the small minority have no rights or privileges over the enormous majority, because the giving of such would lead to immediate disaster. But the majority will not always see in this a reason, nor the minority either, for being for ever mere cyphers and pawns in their own country. They will deem it a mere excuse for always being taxed and ruled in petty things as well as in great, and moved about, at the pleasure of a force over which they have no control. The other result would be the ultimate breaking off of every individual nationality and people to form separate states. We have seen much of this lately in Europe, due to a natural reaction against tyrannous and unsympathetic rule. But either result is to be lamented. Are peoples always to be opposed to one another because they happen not to be of the same race or colour? The savage likes to live apart, and he makes no progress. Where civilisation has been most retarded, it is in those places where a similar social system, but doubtless somewhat modified by time and circumstances, has been practised. The present system of bureaucratic despotism, because of the force behind it, brings peace and order, and in some cases the people are fairly prosperous; but it does not, and cannot, bring a sound and lasting civilisation ; and it does not, and will not, consolidate and strengthen the British Empire.

Fortunately for England, she has not always followed this system. Had she done so Canada would to-day no longer be a portion of the British Empire. The French Canadians are loyal and trustworthy because they have equal rights with others. How comes it that the people of Alsace and Lorraine are almost more passionately French than the French themselves ? Because after the conquest of these countries by France they were so liberally and sympathetically treated by Frenchmen, and made so a part of France not only by duties to be performed but by rights to be enjoyed, that, although to this day the language of the people is as German as their race is, they prefer to be a part of France, and will probably continue of that mind, although now re-united to the old fatherland. How comes it that the Austrian division of partitioned Poland is loyal to the Hapsburgs when the Russian and Prussian divisions hate and execrate their masters ? Because the Austrians give the Galicians rights equal to their own, not in name only but in reality, and the other two powers deny to the Posens and others even the few privileges of their despotic rule. Enough instances can be supplied, from the history of mankind and of Empires, to show that it is not merely impolitic but that it is dangerous for a state to be guided by such narrow views.

Unless an administration be founded on constitutional principles, however just and perfect may be its actions at any epoch, it can never give liberty. But this is a negative objection only. The positive objection comes later on. There is a tendency everywhere for the functions of government to extend themselves, and, by the force of circumstances, the administration becomes an irresponsible bureaucracy—the heaviest handed and most far-reaching of all despotisms—unless countervailing influences exist. The necessities of the times, therefore, in those countries which claim to be governed on constitutional principles, is to extend the forms of local self-government as much as possible, and to decentralise all administrative power and functions that are not required to be concentrated for general purposes. By acting thus the nation continues free and the people maintain their individuality and power of development as much as in any period. The greater action of the administration being more distributed, and being more participated in by the whole people, will strengthen the state without infringing upon, or curtailing, individual rights. The same principle which is good in England is good everywhere else in the Empire, in its due measure and proportion. There will then be the same life-blood flowing throughout. There will be the just emulation of the parts to equal one another, because then it will be possible for them to do so.

There is no record of a people being made better, or developing any superior characteristic that would not have otherwise appeared, by being held in subjection. Of course by the term subjection is not understood that reasonable and necessary subjection to law and order without which no organised society can be strong, or even exist. The term "subjection," in the political sense intended, means being ruled, in minor as well as in great matters, by an outside authority over whose actions the ruled have no power of control. The danger, also, to a free people, of having within its dominions a large number of dependencies which are ruled on different principles to those by which they are themselves ruled is an enormous one but one that is often overlooked. It is not only a manifest danger to the Empire in case of trouble, but it is a danger to freedom. Spain was comparatively a free country before she reached the height of her power, and what the unthinking deem also the acme of her glory. The Imperial instincts bred of despotic rule over widespread dependencies fatally led to the downfall of the local self-governments hitherto enjoyed by the provinces of Spain. The people got to be so accustomed to irresponsible despotic sway, by seeing it in use everywhere almost, that the most disastrous encroachments on their own liberties became possible, and were submitted to, eventually. Spain fell. If she ever again becomes a power it will certainly not be owing to a clipping of the wings of liberty anywhere. Great Britain has also widespread dependencies, almost all of which—in the subdivision here spoken of—are ruled quite as despotically as those of

Spain were, less the cruelty which belonged to another age. There are strong indications, happily, that the struggle between the two influences will have a different result, because the grain of liberty in the British race is too strong to be overcome by these outside influences. Instead of losing their own local iberties they will extend the principle, and establish local self-government in the several dependencies of the Empire, as circumstances may warrant.

With the exception of Barbados, and, to a much more limited degree, of the Bahamas, the people of the British West Indian colonies have no real connection with the public administration; and by the term "administration" is understood not simply those political matters which Governments chiefly have to do with, nor even those smaller matters which local communities and bodies sometimes hand over to a central authority to be dealt with by it, in a uniform manner, for the general good; in this connection the term "administration" means everything pertaining to the common weal of the colonies, from the cleansing out of a village gutter to the fortification of a fort; from the eleemosynary aid given to a starving peasant on the roadside to the pensioning of a high official. In everything—in great things as in small—there is only one centre of legislative and executive administration in these colonies; that one centre is composed of the Governor and his officials, all under the direct orders of Downing Street. Sometimes an Assembly or Council is added, composed partly of officials and partly of members nominated by the administration, or of officials and elected members, but in either case the official vote usually predominates. The people are only called upon to supply the taxes. The internal and domestic affairs of the community are, for all practical purposes, regulated by an arbitrary, an outside, an imperious power, acting on its own lights and on its own lines, and whether the people approve or do not approve of any of the acts done on their behalf, there is really no authoritative means of ascertaining. We only know that the opinion of the people is not duly considered in the matter after the constitutional methods known to Englishmen. The numerous authorities that have the real power—those who make and those who apply the laws and local regulations, in the name of the Crown of the United Kingdom—do as they deem fit after their own judgment. The intervention of a local council, when there is one, is more often than not a mere constitutional device, whose chief purpose seems to be to make it appear that the people have a voice, when really they have none, in the management of their own concerns. Some local parochial Boards recently created in Jamaica are, for all purposes of real local Self-government, more a device than a reality.

There are those, no doubt, who honestly believe that the people of the British West Indies are governed in accordance with certain approved methods which have been adopted after debate in the Parliament of the United Kingdom, or, at least, which have been duly considered in the councils of the Crown at home, and where the views and interests of the several sections of West Indian society have been previously heard, at least by deputy or by commission. But this is not so of those colonies now under consideration. For them no item of legislation was ever debated or even considered anywhere by any truly representative body or council. The legislation given them may have been good, the bye-laws made for them may have been excellent, the administration of both may have been admirable, but the legislation is passed, the bye-laws are imposed, and the administration is worked, arbitrarily ; there are no constitutional means of ascertaining whether the majority of the people approve of the legislation or of the bye-laws, or are satisfied with how they are worked.

Every Act which operates, in the colonies referred to, has been originated by some official or other individual, no doubt, but who he was, or why he thought such legislation useful or applicable, may be, and often is, practically unknown to the body of the people. The local administrators and officials are themselves merely the mouthpieces and pawns of higher administrative powers unconnected with the localities. These latter have views of their own, and whatever those views of the moment may be, they get embodied in Acts, which are passed by the local councils of the several colonies as a matter of course. It is quite possible also, in fact, in course of time, it has got to be known in many instances to be so, that the initiative of enactments and laws may be traced to individuals in temporary local power or holding office transiently, and who have thus a rare opportunity not only of ventilating, but of putting into actual practice, their theories on diverse matters, at the expense of the people. A Governor, also, who has done good service in a colony he happened to know something about, will continue to have the ear of Downing Street, and when he is transferred to another colony he knows nothing about, he may forward to the Secretary of State a despatch enclosing the draft of a pet law of his, which he has persuaded his Colonial Secretary, or Queen's Advocate, or some other high official, to draw up for him. The draft Act is probably sent back from London with an intimation that the views set forth in it may be embodied in a formal Act. The Act is then put into form and submitted to the local council and passed by it as a matter of course, and again it is forwarded to Downing Street for final approval. It is returned approved of, for the ground had been already cleared, and it is then law. Here we have a measure emanating from an official brain—but it is sometimes altered in details by the authorities in Downing Street—and the astonished colonists have to act up to it, trusting that some good, hidden to their obtuse intelligence, may lay embodied in it somewhere.

These measures have nowhere had any opportunity of being subjected to real discussion as understood in Great Britain, or in the Parliamentary colonies. The few non-official members of the local councils (nominated by the administration, or elected), when they do object to any measure put before them, or to any part of any measure, have not the power to hinder its passing. Obvious and glaring errors they no doubt often do arrest, but only because the officials in charge of the measure fall in with non-official views. As a matter of fact, therefore, some measures that have become law have been modified by the non-official views. But many measures that are forced through the councils by the official-administrative vote contain clauses the non-official members, and more often still the general public, deem to be injurious to the best interests of the people, or find to be vexatious in practice and unwarranted in principle. There is no guarantee whatever that the public interest or the people's view of the matter shall receive any consideration whatever. The authority and the power in nearly all local assemblies and councils, for all practical purposes of government, lie exclusively with the officials. The non-official element is practically never more than consultative; and even then it is so only when the official element deems it fit or expedient to consult it.

Now, mark the workings, wheels within wheels, of this exotic despotism in free England itself. Efforts have sometimes been made, emanating from these dependencies—alas ! vain efforts—to break down the barriers erected in them against progress, intelligence, and enlightenment. At first sight one would say the efforts must have been successful, for there was everything to warrant success : the demands of the people of the petitioning dependency were reasonable to demonstration, they were supported by nearly all the wealth and intelligence of the place, they had been discussed in public meetings and in the local press, their obviousness, their undoubted, even their unquestioned, usefulness, could not be gainsaid on the spot. The Governor and his officials could say nothing openly against the demand of the petitioners ; they were too moderate, too reasonable, and too useful, to make it possible to say aught against them —on the spot. The demand, of course, was for the granting of some local power and authority to deal with certain local matters that had been always neglected, to the great loss of the public. Nearly every petition of any importance is of this nature. The petitioners are sanguine men ; men with a good cause often are. They believe in English liberty and in English justice. Perhaps a Liberal Government is in office, and the Colonies have a statesman for chief whose speeches have left nothing to be desired—while he was in opposition. But all this avails nothing. Even if the Governor and his officials do not secretly report against the terms of the petition : to the effect that although there is nothing to be said against it the granting of it would be a dangerous precedent, that other petitions would follow, that there was no local machinery to carry out the views of the petitioners even if they were otherwise excellent. In fact, if the usual machinery is not put in motion by the Governor, on the spot, in order to obstruct the passing of this measure of local self-government, the agencies in England itself are certain to kill it. These agencies are those influences which have been already described. They are active influences, ever at work ; honestly, as they think, and laboriously working to keep matters in the old groove. They believe they are doing their duty. They imagine that the empire, if it is to be upheld in its integrity,

must remain without these changes. Alas! the greatest
enemies of British power could not act more surely or more
maliciously for its ultimate, its inevitable, break up.   It has
been shown that these influences are powerful in commerce, in
industry, in society, in Parliament, and in the Cabinets of
Ministers. It has been seen that the influence is, on the whole,
an evil influence; and it is evil because it is un-English, and
un-English because it runs counter to the genius of the English
people, and saps the foundation of that constitutional liberty
on which the mighty edifice of British power and stability is
constructed.

Nations, as well as individual people, are born into the
world who seem destined to be the special instruments of an
inscrutable Providence.   If elected to accomplish great deeds,
and empire be written on its brow, how, as with the Jews of
old, if the nation prove unworthy?   How, if, instead of dealing
justly, and honourably, and righteously, with God's people, they
debase all to serve some petty ends, some meaner object, it
may even be some sinister purpose?   The greatness of England is her justice, and the splendour of her fame is her liberty.
When she swerves from either of these beacon lights, which, on
the whole, have guided her through the darkness of things, the
shock is felt throughout the empire, as when a ship strikes a
rock.   If England ever falls it will be because she sails away
from this guidance, and follows the old old methods that have
carried to ruin and to degradation so many empires.

The greatness of the British race has been achieved by
diverse methods, but the acquisitions have to a great extent
been safeguarded by a characteristic quality.   If the individual
Englishman measures himself by a moderately big standard he
ever uses a lesser one in public matters, and is always reasonable when acting in consort with his fellows.   Some Continental
people use immoderate measures always.   Those who measure
falsely are not likely to go right.   How can a people know
where they stand, or how can they truly gauge a position, or
measure the difficulties of an enterprise, if they over-estimate
their own strength and capacities, and, in an equal proportion,
under-estimate the merits of other people?   This is a reason,
also, why Englishmen so often win on those occasions where
success seemed otherwise doubtful, if not improbable.   They
are not depressed by overwhelming odds against them, because

they are constitutionally in the habit of always doing their best on every occasion. Due to not having over-measured their strength and capacity, they always put forth their utmost powers to win. They do not expect to win on any other conditions. They are, therefore, always ready for the occasion, however tough it may prove itself. This characteristic quality, added to a constitutional love of justice and almost unclouded traditions of liberty, has not only materially aided the British race in achieving greatness, but has enabled them to retain it. But the world changes, and the relative positions of people towards one another change, and as each change occurs the qualities demanded of Empire must be remodelled to meet the new circumstances. Empires which fail do not remodel except where forced to do so. And as they are being perpetually so forced they strike no roots ; they float along buffeted by storms and the adversaries to which eventually they have to give ground, until they get finally engulfed and disappear for ever from the scene. The lesson has occurred often.

If anarchy nearly invariably follows the downfall of despotisms, it has also sometimes followed the granting of liberty, and, therefore, people are not so sure as they might otherwise be that liberty is always good. No Englishman believes that despotism is good in itself, but many are taught by our bureaucratic Imperialists that it is necessary for those people who have never known any other form of rule, and for people who are unfitted by want of experience in working liberal institutions. They say these people would not know how to properly make use of liberal institutions. Herein lies the whole question. People are given to believe off-hand what they are told by experts, although it comes to their knowledge every day that no one is more apt to make mistakes about some subjects as the expert is. It is not altogether the fault of the expert in this case either ; too much is demanded of him. He is asked for, and he is expected to give, a categorical reply always on a matter whose complexity is not only great, but the materials of which it is constituted are ever shifting and ever changing. It does not always occur to people that the opinion of this political expert is only valuable when taken in conjunction with, and when weighed alongside, the opinions of those who have been long familiar with the particular case to be dealt with. It saves, however, a deal of trouble to call in the expert and take his opinion on the

matter, and then to act up to it.   But Empires are not kept
together without trouble and labour.   The opinion of the
political expert (in this instance the bureaucratic Imperialist)
undoubtedly saves much immediate trouble, and causes endless
complaints and petitions to be pigeon-holed and thrown aside
or met by the stereotyped answer.   Sometimes his opinion is
a true one, and sufficiently meets the case for the moment.
More often the discontent is allowed to remain and to breed in
the dependency.   The discontent is rarely met, rarely overcome; it is sometimes turned aside for a time, or quieted by a
vague promise, but it surely wakes up again more angry than
ever, for having been misled.   It does not occur to the body
of Englishmen that perhaps this political expert is wrong after
all ; that the people in question have known liberty in local
self-government in the days long ago, and that, whether they
did so or not, they are quite fitted for it now.

They are fitted for it now, that is the point.   There are few
people in the world who are not fitted for local self-government
of some kind.   The real question is not the unfitness for it
but the amount of it demanded.   An outward show of political
despotism is not the measure of everything, no more than an
outward show of freedom is.   Even Russia, despotic Russia,
possesses forms of local self-government, and, to a lesser extent,
a reality of it also, which our most enlightened and progressive
dependencies would be only too glad to have, but which our
bureaucratic Imperialists would turn pale and tremble at the
mere mention of giving them.

The inhabitants of the British West Indian colonies do not
ask for now, and never have asked for, any form of local self-
government which they had not all the necessary appliances
for carrying on.   They do not ask, and never have asked, for
any form of local government that could be deemed in any
way inconsistent with British supremacy, or that would interfere
with the proper control of the central government or the pre-
rogatives of the Crown.   Those who sneer at the " local popularities" for desiring to have distributed among themselves
and their friends the positions of emolument, distinction, and
authority, in the several communities of which they are the
local leaders, are sneering at a very common human sentiment
indeed, and which may be found, very fully developed, in the
breasts of Englishmen at home, from the holders of the posts of

Ministers of State through all the countless grades of Government service—the church, the bar, the army, the navy, and the civil service—to the humble porter in the hall. It is an honourable ambition, and, moreover, it is one which, when properly regulated, is of great service to a State.

It is unnecessary here to develop all the particular reasons why the West Indians demand local self-government. If ever there were places in the world requiring it, most assuredly they could not more urgently require it than these dependencies. The mismanagement of local matters has reached such a pitch, notwithstanding the relatively enormous outlay of the people's taxes, that the want of local prosperity may be traced to it in the several islands.

It is a curious coincidence that with the downfall of that gross materiality which our bureaucratic Imperialists so vainly strove to shore up—that gross materiality we must call it, for it was founded on slavery and the degradation of man's highest intelligence—there has been a rise of intellectual life, and an immense appreciation of the advantages of a better moral standard of existence, for the West Indian people. It is not that faint glimmer of an ideal life which almost every community, however low it may be in civilisation, continues to let flicker on among the very few that think, and which even these British dependencies, during the old *régime*, continued to entertain to this extent. It is a dawning light of power, as when the sun in his strength shoots its golden beams from behind the horizon and gilds the clouds of the dawn of a new day. Christianity and education is not doing its work in vain; it never did, and it never will.

But this rising into a new and better life of these old colonies, so long degraded and so deeply engulfed, has demonstrated to the people the advantages and even the necessity of a more widespread and searching system of education. Knowing also that a well-regulated material prosperity must ever accompany a sound and lasting moral progress, the people demand that their taxes shall also supply technical schools, agricultural colleges, and so forth. The withdrawal of the wealth brought by high-priced sugar has caused some leanness and hunger among the resident middle classes and the people, but it has also led to a spirit of inquiry, and a general movement, that is making its way surely to a sounder and healthier state of things for these colonies than was ever known, or dreamt of for them, before. The fall of the powerful monopoly, the big planter, and the princely merchant, will continue to be deplored by our bureaucratic Imperialists, but it is more than compensated for by the gradual and certain rise of the great bulk of the people from the condition of ill-fed, and, may be, contented freedmen, bordering on the lowest and most abject stages of human existence, into the condition of a civilised, Christian, educated, and self-respecting peasantry. Instead of the old condition of things from which we all willingly avert our eyes, we see arising before us a people of moral worth, possessing a sense of those higher aims and obligations, which a performance of Christian religious duties, and of family obligations, and a recognised position in the state, together with a love of organised liberty, must always yield.

We hear ceaselessly of the ruin of the West Indies, but this simply means the break up of the old order of things. The new order of society which is being evolved contains elements of stability which were missing. The establishment of a large body of peasant owners and a number of middle-class cultivators alongside a few great proprietors cannot reasonably be accounted a calamity in any country. There are certain interests—the interests of merchant monopolists, which are powerful because they possess influence at Downing Street —who appear to dislike the change for the reasons that they expect they will lose by it. They fear a change in the course of trade. It is doubtless a misfortune to see any interest in a country suffer loss, but in this instance those who suffer have only themselves to blame. It is their own folly, not the new proprietary, that has killed them. Had they acted with reasonable foresight, had they been equal to the duties of their position in a measure somewhat commensurate with the rights they claimed, they might not only have held but have even strengthened their position. The new middle class would have but filled up the void that always lay dangerously open between the large proprietors and the mere labourers—the recent slaves. The evolution is now in full progress, but it will take time to complete itself. One result will be the dethronement of the sugar-cane in the sense of its being almost the only product raised for export, and the adoption in its place of various kinds of marketable produce cultivated by resident owners of the soil. Monopolists, doubtless, will have little field here, and from their point of view the old times may well be regretted. We have thus on the spot a growing power best fitted of all for the duties of local self-government—a power, missing for over a century, whose absence has been the main cause of West Indian difficulties. But this backbone of every civilised community, whose advent must be welcomed by well-wishers to these dependencies, by no means shuts out the large proprietor, the capitalist, or the company. If it were inevitable that the two could not live together, that one class must give way to the other, then of course the thousands of small resident cultivators must be preferred to the few big ones. But in the new and better order of civilisation that is being established in these dependencies the old notions will happily find no place ; the usual gradations of society found in every advanced community will be established.

The system that may have suited a state of things represented by an absentee proprietary holding nearly all the best lands, and a servile or semi-servile labouring class working under them, does not, and cannot, in any way suit that other and very different state of things which is represented by a numerous local body of men who own the land and work it themselves, who reap the profit themselves, and who pay all the taxes.

We are therefore confronted in the West Indies, at the present moment, with a difficulty, due to this change in the circumstances of the people, and unless it be openly met in a statesmanlike manner, by the granting of proper forms of local self-government, there will be discontent and its consequences. Chief among these consequences will be a want of confidence and a want of credit, followed by a want of a feeling of stability. We know that all this may lead to lawlessness. The remedy, therefore, is obvious. The illness was due to mismanagement ; and this mismanagement will continue unless the people themselves are empowered to manage their own local concerns.

Mr. Froude says the Australians and New Zealanders will not be found enthusiastic for the extension of self-government in the West Indies when they know that it means the extinction of their own white brothers who have settled there. It is more than likely the Australians and New Zealanders will be indifferent to the whole matter, but, should it happen to be otherwise, it is to be hoped for their own sakes they will read the times aright, and not interpose at all unless they are prepared to aid the West Indian people in obtaining a measure of that liberty to which they owe everything themselves. There are colonists of note who appear in London occasionally who are strong upholders of bureaucratic Imperialism for every dependency, and who, for aught we know, would prefer some less liberal form of government for their own colonies than obtains in them. But these colonists who come to London with these views do not express them in the colonies they live in, and, even if they did, it would really not matter, because they would be so minute a minority of the people that no one would pay attention to them. The white brothers of the New Zealanders have diminished to a tenth of the number they were fifty years ago in the West Indies under a form of government which no ingenuity of language can call otherwise than despotic. It has simply been a bureaucratic despotism under the thumb of Downing Street, and in which the blacks, so far, have had no political or social influence whatever. Should the Australians and New Zealanders desire to see the remnant of their white brothers leave the West Indies for good, they have only to pray for the imposition of Mr. Froude's *régime*. The astute among them might be disposed to do this in the hope of attracting some of the runaways to their own colony. As a matter of fact and of history the white population of the West Indies has the most frequently and the most loudly complained of the want of local self-government; the black population, as Mr. Froude justly remarks, have been less eager for change. Poor things! they were slaves, and they have been emancipated; they like the British connection, and will take from Great Britain the form of government vouchsafed them. Besides, the opinion of the black man is not easy to get at. He will give it openly and fairly to any man if he feels he could do so without risk to himself and his belongings from the powers that be, or even were he certain that his doing so would serve any useful purpose. The black man knows that if he gives any views of his own which are in any way opposed to the local governments at present existing he will probably be made to feel it hereafter. An abundant experience has also shown him that Royal Commissions, and all that, invariably end in nothing practical being done to alter the *status quo*. He therefore keeps his counsel. The white man is less philosophical and less resigned ; he frets and fumes ; and if he be really a clever man and might turn out to be a dangerous one to the existing bureaucratic Imperial *régime*, efforts, not always unsuccessful, are made to bring him within its folds by the offer of a snug place.

Mr. Froude's book bristles with theories which are thoroughly and characteristically inconsistent with one another. He also says that it is fear of the allegiance of the West Indian whites that has induced Downing Street to take in hand these dependencies for the purpose of conferring on them liberal institutions. He says the British black man would greatly dislike seeing his islands admitted into the American Union, but that the Englishman in the West Indies hopes almost against hope for this consummation of all his desires. Downing Street, therefore, will grant local self-government to these dependencies, feeling a comfortable assurance that the British black man will keep his white brother in order, and not permit him to stray away from the path of loyalty.

Mr. Froude also says the English in the West Indies desire to be adopted by the United States to save them from the black domination they fear. But there are weekly meetings of the English in the West Indies asking for local self-government ; there has never yet been one asking for union with the States. Mr. Froude always knows what people want better than they do themselves. Would the West Indian dependencies under the United States flag be less free than they are now ? No one dare say that. A union of any kind or under any conditions with the United States would mean freedom in the sense of the fullest possible local self-government. The United States has no machinery wherewith to govern despotically. She could not take over a West Indian colony unless she did so as a " territory," with full local self-government in its widest sense. The English in the West Indies would like the transfer from this point of view, doubtless, but from no other. It is doubtful, however, whether these dependencies are fitted yet for such a great privilege, and such an extended liberty. None of them ever asked for so much, or anything approaching it, and no one ever did it on their behalf. But we all know that under the Stars and Stripes a well-regulated liberty, equal for

all, and firmly held according to the constitution, would be
certain for these dependencies.   Every man in the West Indies
feels and knows this, both white and black.   But they think
and feel, also, that the same may be accomplished under the
British flag.   And why not?   Is not Great Britain the parent
of liberty and well-ordered freedom everywhere except in her
own dependencies?   Were the British West Indies, owing to
fortuitous circumstances, ever to fall under the flag of the
United States, we should all doubtless admire the virile and
vigorous handling they would receive.   But it would be the
moulding of another figure of liberty.   It would be another
addition to the world of a free centre for men to live and
grow in, not the poor, puny, manacled, thing Mr. Froude and
his friends would give us.

CHAPTER XII.

THE term "West Indies" is a geographical expression, and not a very happy one, denoting certain territories, some British, some belonging to foreign powers, and some independent. The term is usually confined to the archipelago of islands lying between North and South America, but sometimes the dependencies of England in Central America and on the southern mainland are included. The archipelago north of Cuba, known as the Bahamas, is also embraced by the designation. Other countries give other names; the French call the latter group the Lucayes, and the first-mentioned archipelago the Great and Little Antilles.

It would serve a purpose to have a name which would designate the British possessions, as a whole, exclusive of all foreign possessions; and for this purpose a good Anglo-Saxon term might have been coined had not a good local name existed on the spot, which serves the double object of conveying the political and geographical meaning intended to be conveyed, and, at the same time, calls to mind the historic past in the now extinct Carib races. The various European powers found these Caribs occupying most of the islands when they first took possession of them, but they all aided in destroying them. The few that remain owe their survival to the inaccessibility of the localities they dwelt in.

It is proposed to call the whole British West Indies by the name, "The Caribbean Confederation."

It will comprise the following British Island Governments:—

Antigua (with Barbuda); The Bahamas archipelago; Barbados; Dominica; Grenada (with part of the Grenadines); Jamaica (with Turks and Caicos Islands); St. Kitts-Nevis (with Anguilla) ; St. Lucia ; Montserrat ; Tobago ; Trinidad ; St. Vincent (with the remainder of the Grenadines) ; The Virgin Islands. Added to these will be the two mainland governments—Guiana on the South American mainland, and Honduras in Central America.

The people occupying these several dependencies have been referred to in previous chapters. It will not be necessary to say much more about them here. The English and African races are the two on which the future practically rests. The Coolies are East Indians, and are too few to make any change in the course of events as they are shaping themselves. Besides, their interests, on the whole, will be similar to those of the English and Africans. They are a numerous body in Trinidad and Guiana. It has yet to be seen whether they will increase in numbers or grow fewer when left to themselves, without fresh importations of their number from the East. Their social habits are, as yet, unaltered. In course of time they will probably become Christians. A good many are Mohammedans, and it is even said this religion is making proselytes in the West Indies. This is a question worth study by those of Mr. Froude's way of thinking. If the Mohammedan religion could be introduced into Hayti, to replace Paganism and the Christianity established there, the Africans might take to it as kindly as they do in Africa. Being Mohammedans, salted baby would go the way of salted pork, and we should never again hear of the article being distributed among worshippers. One advantage would be that the haters of progressive liberty and of local self-government would have to abandon this well-worked-up and much-used scarecrow, and leave the people of our British dependencies to work out their own salvation, without perpetually introducing it as a warning to frighten away liberty, and perpetuate the paternal guidance of the bureaucratic Imperialist, or the gentle hand and the sweet unchecked will of the Rajah Brooks of the future with which Mr. Froude and his friends would endow them.

Fortunately for these countries, civilisation and Christianity are rapidly gaining ground, not only in the British dependencies, but in the foreign West Indies also, and even in San Domingo and Hayti. The greatest and most rapid advance is being made in the dependencies of Great Britain, due chiefly, if not entirely, to the disinterested and meritorious efforts of independent religious bodies. These bodies are surely and unostentatiously laying the basis of a sound Christianity, and a sound civilisation of the highest grade ; fitting the people for the rights and duties of British citizens.

The East Indian as a man is better known than the African ; he represents an old, an effete, a bygone civilisation. Physically he is a weakling alongside of the African, who is always strong and often herculean ; as a social unit in the world the African, also, will probably surpass the East Indian before many years have elapsed. The African has no prejudices to overcome ; he takes a common-sense view of a situation ; he acts up to the necessities imposed on him ; he has no impedimenta of past ages to encumber his advance and act as a drag on his progress. In pages 364-5, Vol. I., of that interesting work, " Three Thousand Miles through Brazil," by James W. Wells, the following statement is made :—

" In spite of all that has been written and said of the indolence of the negro, I find that in the interior of Brazil the free black is *the* working-man ; the pure negroes are by far the most intelligent and industrious of the inhabitants. I could not possibly wish for a better *camarado* than my black *tropeiro* Chico ; he was skilful, attentive, respectful, honest, and obliging, but black as coal, and the blacker a.negro is, so is he proportionately trustworthy."

The Queen has a million and a half of black subjects in the West Indies, and in all Her Majesty's dominions there are none more truly loyal and devoted to the throne. The circumstances of these dependencies have been such that everything men most prize has come to the black people direct from England ; they owe nothing, in this way, to the islands of their birth. They love their islands because their homes are in them, but all the civil rights they possess have been given them rather against the wishes and advice of their old local governors and masters than by their favour. They owe these nothing ; to England they owe everything, and they therefore venerate the memory of the great men she produced —the men who worked for the rights and liberties of their race.

The Colonial Office, also, has done some good service to the blacks in recent times, by insisting on the white and coloured races being deemed equal whenever their capacities

are equal.   Among local employés, blacks and half-castes have
equal shares with local whites under the existing régime.   The
outside influences that have been so mischievous in these
colonies have been due perhaps more to parliamentary pressure,
and back-stairs political influences with ministers, than to the
initiative of the Colonial Office, although, of course, the office
gets debited with all the bad.   One of the great faults of the
present system is that there can be no guarantee, that at any
future time, some powerful outside influences may not again be
brought to bear on a minister who, for general political reasons,
will sacrifice the interest of the dependency entrusted to him.
Such things have been done before now, and why not again?
The British merchants found means to compel the ministers
for the colonies to sacrifice the resident landed gentry of the
West Indian Islands, and the local agricultural interest generally, to their special interests.   Vast sums were unjustly, un-
constitutionally, and arbitrarily forced from the people of
Ceylon to help to meet military deficits elsewhere ; and important local works which these monies had been accumulated
to build had to be given up, to the great and permanent loss of
the people of this colony.   Nearly every Crown colony has one
or more such tales in its poor history.

The universal demand for more local self-government is not
due to a want of loyalty to British rule, but to a well-founded
feeling that progress is hardly practicable without it.   A people
can be made loyal, and they can be kept loyal, by granting to
them their just demands.   The withholding of these demands
always endangers loyalty and sometimes destroys it, notwithstanding that the demands first promulgated have subsequently
been granted, and perhaps even much more.   How a thing is
given, and when, makes a great difference.   Administrators
who are unaware of this fact, or who under-estimate the sentiment that lies beneath the facts of life, are unworthy to have
power in any empire, especially in one where the races differ
from one another in their origin, their character, and their
history.

It can be fairly said of the English in the West Indies—
those who reside in and have an interest in the dependencies
as proprietors, merchants, and professional men—that they are
cordially desirous and willing to see the same liberty given to
the coloured people they demand for themselves.   The olden

times are gone, and the old ideas that belonged to them are rapidly following. The survivals only serve as reminiscences or curiosities which need not be considered by practical men; they have little.influence on passing events, and will have none on the future.

Local legislative reforms, including the creation of Municipalities, were alluded to in the Reports of the Royal Commission on certain West Indian islands, published in 1884. But the recommendations practically left the authority in the hands of the officials, by giving the nominative vote, as a rule, power enough in number to swamp the elective vote. Under such conditions, the creation of local bodies would be a useless formality for all ordinary purposes of local self-government; it would lead to unseemly disputes, as may be too often seen now in similar cases, and little else. Give the right thing or nothing. The people are either fitted for local self-government in these matters or they are not. If they are fitted for it, give it; if they are not fitted for it, withhold it. But a sham will always be mischievous.

In the accompanying sketch of the fifteen separate islands and mainland governments which constitute the British West Indies, great differences will be found to exist in the forms of local self-government. The reasons for these differences are historical, and are well known, and can be readily accounted for. But no valid reason whatever can be given now why every one of the fifteen colonies should not enjoy the same measure of local self-government possessed by the most favoured. The constitution possessed by Barbados, with one or two slight alterations, might be made the basis of a local self-government for each of the fifteen colonies. There is a great amount of ignorance afloat about the local governments possessed by these colonies in the anti-emancipation days and for some years subsequent. People are given to say many of these colonies had local self-government once, but abrogated their rights because they found a bureaucratic despotism suited them better. To say this is historically untrue and morally a falsehood. Some who give forth this opinion know better; but political exigency, or political reasons of some kind, make men say things they would not otherwise say; it even makes them sometimes disavow their convictions. Whatever be the reasons—whether they be due to ignorance or due to political expediency—they have no bottom. Every one of the British West Indian islands, with the exception of Trinidad and St. Lucia, have had elective representative Assemblies, and in their day they fully represented the free citizens of the several islands. The suffrage was regulated to meet the wants of the oligarchy of white planters. But when the Act of Emancipation made the slaves free, these Assemblies represented interests that were antagonistic to the bulk of the people, and that were even opposed to the new ideas of the Home Government. After a time, the Home Government, instead of placing these Assemblies on a footing compatible with the social changes brought about by emancipation and other circumstances, and thereby making them again workable, deemed it a good opportunity to abolish them. It was impossible for any one, however liberally inclined he might be, to stand up for these Assemblies, which now only represented a minute oligarchy, and they, therefore, nearly all gradually disappeared—under pressure, and the usual administrative methods employed for such purposes. The Barbados Assembly, instead of being abolished, as so many others were, has been reformed, and no one can stand up and say that, from every point of view, Barbados has not greatly profited. Why Barbados escaped the sad fate of the other islands is unknown. It was always a rich island, and like rich people it had no doubt some powerful interests that had to be reckoned with. The Leeward Islands had a sad fate indeed. They were asked to confederate, and, all the world over, confederation usually confers strength. They had each little Assemblies of their own, with elective elements that were not very valuable, but they could have easily been made most valuable by reform. Some of these islands were induced to surrender their elective Assemblies and local self-governments. When they were confederated they found themselves bound up together, no doubt, but their heads, feet, and hands had been chopped off. They found themselves all welded and hammered together into a single government, with a pure bureaucratic despotism at the head. The word "confederation" was never before, perhaps, in the history of the world, used for such a purpose. Confederation means the possession of local self-government by the several constituent parts, and a general government for the purposes of all; any other use of the term is a misnomer.

Taking the fifteen colonies, their united public revenues from all sources and for all purposes in 1886 was £2,062,563, of which £883,675 was levied by import duties of customs, or over 42½ per cent. A large proportion of these duties were raised on necessary articles of food imported for popular use. There is little doubt that with a more representative form of government these onerous and disastrous forms of taxation would be soon much mitigated, and in course of time probably removed. There are also duties on exportable produce in some of the colonies. With present markets a worse form of taxation could not be. There are extreme occasions in which taxation of exports may be allowable, but they are rare, and the imposition should never be more than temporary. The total exports of the fifteen colonies for the year 1887 were valued at £7,606,169, of which £3,198,302 were shipped to the United Kingdom; £3,877,453 to foreign countries; and £530,414 to other colonies. The total imports for the year 1886 were valued at £7,314,492, of which £2,888,236 were British; £3,315,279 foreign; and £1,110,977 from other colonies. The exports for 1887 are less in value but not in quantity compared with recent years. There is a proportionate lessening in the value for imports. The public debts were £2,829,338. There were 173 miles of railway, and 1,034 miles of telegraph only. About one in nine of the whole population attend school. At the close of the year 1886 the population was officially estimated to be 1,510,014. It was probably more than this; it is now probably about 1,560,000.

The revenue of £2,062,563 has to serve for all purposes. In some of the colonies—like Barbados, Jamaica, Trinidad, Guiana, Grenada, St. Lucia—there are local authorities who have a limited control over, and sometimes collect, certain small revenues, but in the other colonies the general government of the colony does everything. In any scheme for local self-government, more distinct and more adequately established authorities—such as municipalities—will have to be set up for the towns. The rural districts also will have to be granted certain powers to do those things which rural local authorities are most competent to perform for themselves. In the general scheme for confederation sufficient sums must be set aside for these purposes.

For these fifteen colonies there are now eight governors, all receiving their orders from Downing Street direct, each with his staff, and nine lieutenant-governors, administrators, or presidents, four of whom receive orders from the Governor of the Windward Islands, and five from the Governor of the Leeward Islands. This makes seventeen governors and administrators for the fifteen colonies, because the Windward and Leeward Islands have every one not only their separate administrators, but a governor for each of the two groups. There are ten chief justices and twelve other judges, and the elaborate and costly paraphernalia of numerous supreme courts, besides a large supply of highly-paid magistrates. Each of the eight general governments is supplied with colonial secretaries, collectors of customs, receivers-general, auditors-general, and so on, each with large staffs, duplicating and re-duplicating very expensive, but wholly unnecessary, officials. There are attorneys-general, solicitors-general, and inspectors-general of police, of course ; and heads of public works ; and chiefs of medical departments ; and registrar-generals ; and inspectors-general of education ; and so forth, for each of the eight general governments, all of them with the costly appendages of separate great departments of State ; as if each of these colonies were large, widely distant, rich, and powerful communities, that had nothing in common, and that could never be amalgamated. As may be seen by a perusal of their several conditions and governments in the Blue Books, the nine lieutenant-governorships have also their separate arrangements for duplication and reduplication of numerous offices, the so-called confederations of the Windward and Leeward Islands being mere mockeries ; the only visible thing abolished by the term being the local self-governments, or partly elected Assemblies. which cost nothing. On the contrary, expenditure on official salaries has increased, expenditure for public purposes has decreased, and the condition is more intolerable than it was before. It is true there are two new governors-general that did not before exist. In no country in the world is there anything like the same proportion of the public taxes eaten up by salaries as in these British West Indies. The form of taxation, also, is founded on an elaborate and widespread system of import duties ; always costly to collect, and always injurious to trade and to labour,

PRESENT EXPENDITURE ON THE FIFTEEN WEST INDIAN COLONIES COMPOSING THE SUGGESTED CARIBBEAN CONFEDERATION.

Population, 1,560,000 ; about 122 to the square mile for islands ;
2.4 for Guiana ; and 4 for Honduras.
Attending school, about 166,000, or 1 in 9 of the population.

Administration, including Secretaries and Audit	£94,500
Administration of the Law	137,500
Police and Gaols	253,000
Collection of Revenue	95,000
Ecclesiastical Grants	60,000
Education of the People	105,000
Medical and Hospital Expenditure	220,000
Expenditure on the Poor	80,000
Public Works Departments	320,000
	1,365,000
Steam Communication and Subsidies for Mails and Telegraphs	80,000
Railways, 173 miles, Debentures and Debts	190,000
Post Offices and Savings Banks	67,000
Colonial Military Expenditure—between 2,400 and 3,000 men	30,000
Expenditure on Immigrants (Indian and Chinese indentured labour)	134,200
Contingencies	196,363
	£2,062,563

£1 6s. 4½d. per head of population.

SUGGESTED EXPENDITURE FOR THE GENERAL GOVERNMENT AND THE FIFTEEN LOCAL GOVERNMENTS OF THE CARIBBEAN CONFEDERATION.

Governor-General of the Caribbean Confederation ...	£4,000
Secretaries and A.D.C.	1,000
Lieutenant-Governors of the States of Jamaica, Guiana, Barbados, Trinidad, Bahamas, Grenada, St. Lucia, St. Vincent, St. Kitts-Nevis, Antigua, Dominica, Honduras ; 12 States at £1,000 per annum each	12,000
Lieutenant-Governors of the States of Tobago, Montserrat, Virgin Islands ; 3 States at £800 per annum each	2,400
State Secretaries to the Local Governments of Jamaica, Guiana, Barbados, Trinidad ; 4 at £600 per annum each	2,400
State Secretaries to the Local Governments of Bahamas, Grenada, St. Lucia, St. Vincent, St. Kitts-Nevis, Antigua, Dominica, Honduras ; 8 at £400 per annum	3,200
Carried forward £25,000

Brought forward	£25,000	
State Secretaries to the Local Governments of Tobago, Montserrat, Virgin Islands ; 3 at £200 per annum each	600	
Clerical Aid for the above State Secretaries for the 15 States—distributed in proportion to the work to be done	5,800	
Financial Secretaries to the States of Jamaica, Guiana, Barbados, Trinidad ; 4 at £900 per annum ...	3,600	
(In the other 11 States the State Secretaries will do the duties of Financial Secretaries.)		
Clerical Aid for the Financial Secretaries' Departments of the 15 States	5,800	
(The Lieutenant-Governors and State Secretaries to carry out the Audit work.)		
Government Administration	————	40,800
Collection of Revenue		75,000
(The duties of Collector of Customs, Receiver-General, Treasurer, &c., to be carried on in one office (as a bank might be), under the supervision of the Lieutenant-Governors, State Secretaries, and Financial Secretaries.)		
Supreme Court of Justice ; 3 Judges at £3,000 per annum	9,000	
Resident Judges at Guiana, Jamaica, Trinidad, Barbados ; 4 at £1,500 per annum	6,000	
Resident Judges at Bahamas, Honduras ; 2 at £1,000 per annum	2,000	
2 Leeward Islands and 2 Windward Islands Circuit Judges ; 4 at £1,000 per annum	4,000	
Attorneys-General, Solicitors-General, Public Prosecutors ; by fees	6,000	
Clerks, Bailiffs, &c.	5,500	
Magistracy*	82,500	
Administration of the Law ...	————	115,000
Ecclesiastical Grants		35,000
Education of the People		120,000
Medical and Hospital Expenditure		210,000
Police and Gaols		220,000
Expenditure on the Poor		80,000
Public Works...		263,200
Steam Communications and Subsidies for Mails and Telegraphs		80,000
Railway Debentures and Debts		190,000
Post Offices and Savings Banks		67,000
Military Expenditure		27,000
Expenditure on Immigrants		130,000
Contingencies...		120,000
Carried forward		£1,773,000

* This item is calculated on the present scale, and is open to serious revision,

It is proposed to have a chief responsible officer for each department of government, appointed by the Crown, who will carry out the intentions of the people, expressed through their legislature to the Federal Council. They will transmit the necessary orders, through the Governor-General, to the various Lieutenant-Governors and other officials. They will be *ex-officio* members of both the Upper and Lower Houses. They will be members of the Federal Council. They will propose the measures affecting their departments. They will answer all questions. They will have no right to vote in Assembly or Senate on any measure whatever. They will be the supervisors in chief of the revenues and expenditures of their departments. They will see that the yearly or other returns demanded by the Legislature be duly prepared. These officers will be as follows :—

Brought forward		£1,773,000
The Secretary-General of the Caribbean Confederation, the Treasurer and Receiver-General, the Attorney-General, the Postmaster-General, the Secretary-General for Transport and Mails, the Secretary-General for Education and Public Worship, the Secretary-General for Public Works, the Secretary-General for Hospitals and Poor Relief, the Secretary-General for Police and Gaols ; 9 at £1,200 per annum	10,800	
Clerical Aid ; 9 at £300 per annum	2,700	
		13,500
Total Estimated Expenditure ...		£1,786,500

This expenditure is less by £276,063 than that now expended by the fifteen colonies. The sum of £2,062,563 now expended by these colonies includes all town, municipal, village, and local expenditures, and the like expenditures are included in the estimate for the Caribbean Confederation. The surplus of £276,063 is, therefore, by the figures, a real one. In the scheme of expenditure for the Caribbean Confederation, it will be observed that the only expenditure that it is proposed should be increased is the education vote by £15,000 ; but the increase should be much more considerable. The suggested expenditure for steam communication and subsidies for mails and telegraphs, for post offices and savings banks, and for railway debentures and debts, remains the same as the present expenditure on these items. The ecclesiastical grants are reduced because, as a matter of fact, they are gradually being done away with in several of the present governments. The less expenditures put down for the others is due to the concentration of supervision, the amalgamation of offices, and to simplification of work. In the departments of public works, hospitals, and gaols, the multiplicity of chiefs, and of systems, leads to intolerable expense, immense waste of public money, and great inefficiency. The new system would cause half as much work again to be done for the lesser sums put down.

The subsidies to mail steamers has remained untouched, because it is deemed that transport is, or should be, an affair for private enterprise. Nevertheless, at the first going off, the transport of judges and officials and members of the legislature will have to be carried out regularly and efficiently, and if no private enterprise be forthcoming for the purpose, the Government will have the means at hand of doing the work for itself without loss. Instead of building Government railways, or guaranteeing interest on the railway stock of private companies, as many wholly mainland governments do, it can have steamers of its own, or guarantee a dividend to a private steamship company for a term of years, to carry out the necessary transport between the several States. There is no doubt whatever that the new life and the new movement, which the Caribbean Confederation will bring about, will bring on a state of things that will more likely lead to competition between rival companies for the larger trade and transport of passengers that must necessarily follow, than necessitate any interference of the General Government. Under any circumstances the surplus of £276,063 will leave a margin for transport, and for the buildings, roads, telegraphs, water supplies, and other necessary and urgent public works that have been so long neglected or waited for. A simplification of tariffs, that will assuredly follow on the proposed confederation, would stimulate trade, lessen the weight of taxation on the people, and reduce the cost of collection still further, and lead to an increase of revenue.

The General Assembly of the Caribbean Confederation should be an elective body on the system of proportional representation, in order that the larger States shall not too much overshadow the smaller ones. By the system of proportional representation proposed each State will have its due weight in the General Assembly, but no more. When a State numbers over 400,000 people, let every 15,000 inhabitants send a member; when between 200,000 and 400,000, let every 10,000 inhabitants send one; when between 100,000 and 200,000, let there be a member for every 8,000. Let all the other States have one member for every 6,000 inhabitants. By this method Jamaica—including Turks and Caicos Islands—would have 41 members; Guiana, 27; Barbados, 22; Trinidad, 22; Bahamas, 8; Grenada, 8; St. Kitts-Nevis, 8; St. Vincent, 7; St. Lucia, 7; Antigua (with Barbuda), 6; Honduras, 5; Dominica, 5; Tobago, 3; Montserrat, 2; Virgin Islands, 1. Total, 172 members. This assembly might be elected every three years.

The Senate of the Caribbean Confederation might be elected from among the members of their own bodies by the local assemblies of the fifteen States. The representation in this body would also be proportional as regards the larger States, but each of the smaller States would be represented. This body should be fewer in number; one-quarter the number of the General Assembly would perhaps suffice. In this case the State of Jamaica would send 10 senators; Guiana, 7; Barbados and Trinidad, 5 or 6 each; Bahamas, Grenada, St. Kitts-Nevis, St. Vincent, St. Lucia, and Antigua, 2 each; Honduras, Dominica, Tobago, Montserrat, and the Virgin Islands, 1 each. Total, 46 members. Half this body might be renewed by election every three years. It would thus never be entirely a new body. Those States having only single members, together with the others, might determine by a ballot which of them shall have to re-elect after the first term, after which it would continue to be a matter of rotation.

It is proposed also to have a Federal Council with executive powers. This body to consist of the Governor-General of the Caribbean Confederation as President, the commander of the troops, the 9 Secretaries-General, 10 members by election from among their own body of the General Assembly, and 5 similarly elected members of the Senate. This Federal Council—26 in number—would see to the carrying out of the machinery of government by the officials of the Crown in compliance with the declared wishes of the people through their representatives. The yearly federal budget would require their

assent before being submitted to the Assembly, as well as all
other direct federal money votes.   This Federal Council could
be enlarged into a Federal Tribunal if it ever became necessary to determine disputes between States, or other gravely con-
tentious matters, and questions of constitutional law, by adding
to its ordinary members the judges of the Supreme Court.
The elective members of the Federal Council should be
renewed every three years.

The powers of the General Assembly and Senate are to be
those usually given to Parliament.   They elect their own
officers.   The Governor-General would open the sessions in the
usual way, but have no right to sit, speak, or vote in either
elected House.   The heads of all the departments should be
ex-officio members of both Houses, in order that they may
submit the measures affecting their departments, and answer
questions.   But they are to have no right to vote on any
measure whatever.

The Crown will have the appointment and control of all
the chief public officers, through the Governor-General, who
receives his instructions from the Secretary of State.   The
Governor-General should have the power of veto within certain
prescribed limits.

If, at any time, there be disputes as to the powers of the
General Assembly, the Senate, or any of the local representative bodies, or of any of the States, the Federal Tribunal shall
be called together by the Governor-General to decide as to the
merits of the same.   The Governor-General should have the
power to refer a decision to the Privy Council at home for
approval, revision, or disallowance.

The several local assemblies and councils in the fifteen
units of the Confederacy will have to be created on a representative basis where they do not now exist, and where they do
exist, but on a basis not sufficiently representative for the full
purposes of local self-government, they will have to be remodelled for the purpose.   It is not intended here to lay down
a plan for each of the fifteen States.   It is enough to say that
the several local assemblies should be thoroughly representative, and should have absolute control, within constitutionally
defined limits, over local taxation and expenditure and local
affairs.   It has been already said that Barbados may serve as
an example.   The Lieutenant-Governors will perform towards

these local assemblies almost similar functions to those which the Governor-General will do towards the General Assembly and Senate. They will open the Sessions. But they will also attend the sittings *ex-officio*, as the chiefs of departments do the General Assembly and Senate, to answer questions connected with their duties, and to submit Government propositions, but not otherwise to speak in such assemblies, or to have a vote. These Lieutenant-Governors will have to perform the duties of administrators and colonial secretaries and, at times, of chief auditors of public accounts. They will have to see to the compilation of the serviceable returns so much required, but now often so unattainable, for general information. They should be transferable from State to State as may be determined upon by the Federal Council.

There will be a local executive council required in each State. This council can be composed of the Lieutenant-Governor as president, the State secretary and one or two other officials, as circumstances may warrant, and a few members elected from among their own body by the local assemblies. The elected members of this body should be re-elected every three years.

After the general and local assemblies have elected from among their several bodies the members required to serve in the Federal Senate, the Federal Council, and the Local Executive Councils, the authorities will proceed to have other members elected to the general and local assemblies to take their places.

There will be funds required for the payment of the necessary officials of the General Assembly, the Senate, the Federal Council, and the several local assemblies; but this need not be a large item, and there are ample funds available.

With regard to the apportionment of the revenues raised, the several States will, of course, disburse for their own local benefit the major portions. The cost of the general government and the disbursements for general objects are matters which will lie within the province of the Federal Council, the General Assembly, and the various local assemblies. These matters can only be determined, from time to time, by the circumstances of the situation.

It is unlikely that any one can draw up a scheme in its details that will meet with universal approval. But most people will admit the advantages of a Federation of all the British West Indies into a single powerful colonial State. The feasibility of the project is as beyond doubt as are its advantages. A Caribbean Confederation as described will attract colonists and capital. Englishmen will go to a place where there is a government powerful for good, and where their intelligence, energy, and enterprise will find a fitting reward not only in private but in public life. The English localised in these fifteen dependencies will awake to a new life, because they can see for themselves they will be enabled—as they are not now—to participate in the public life of their countries and help to guide their fortunes. And where are there men who do not see the power of this sentiment in this world? The English in the West Indies are now a numerous but inert body; they will become a more numerous and an active body.

The African, as a man, is out on the prairie; he is under the control of no precedents; he can therefore be moulded more easily than those other races who live in a track so deep-rutted, so time-worn, and so long traversed, that hardly any efforts can get them to leap over the high barriers into the free, open, world outside. Enough has been said in previous chapters to show the excellence of the material, and it will indeed be a blunder if the British Government do not grant to their West Indian colonies, because the African is there, that local self-government of which this African is certain to make good use for the stability and true renown of this empire, as much as any of the other residents.

Jamaica.

At the close of the year 1886, the population of Jamaica was estimated at 620,000, being nearly 148 to the square mile. This included about 12,000 coolies imported by the sugar planters. The females exceed the males by more than 15,000. Less than one-quarter of the land is under cultivation. There is nothing in the climate of Jamaica to cause Englishmen to avoid this splendid island. On the contrary, in this respect, we have no tropical colony to equal it. The climatic conditions of Cuba have not been unfavourable to the white race. Although a little more south than the latter island, Jamaica is, on the whole, more favourably placed. It stands more out in the ocean and faces the free breeze that passes from the North between the high lands of Hayti and Cuba, and is cut off by the latter island from the effects of the sluggish and unhealthy waters of the Mexican Gulf. Untoward circumstances have caused this colony to be comparatively neglected by Englishmen. Chief among the causes must be named that perverse legislation which allowed the British merchants to manipulate the encumbered Estates Court, by which they probably enriched themselves but undoubtedly ruined the prospects of this island for half a century. This subject has been dealt with in the chapter " the English in the West Indies." There is only one way to make a colony worth possessing by a free country, and that way is to encourage settlers who will reside in the colony and cultivate the land for their own profit. Slavery was abolished in Jamaica, as elsewhere, but the social system, of which slavery was only a part, remained. It looks as if a new era was about to dawn for Jamaica as for the other West Indies. The lien of the en· cumbered Estates Court has been abolished, and local self-government is being given to the people. There is a fairly large and a steadily increasing population, and labour of the best kind in the world for agricultural purposes may be relied on— if good wages be given for it. An Englishman with a small capital, ready to work himself, is certain to succeed if he goes to this island in a right frame of mind. He will be close to the United Kingdom, the United States, and, therefore, to the best markets in the world. But if he wants to secure good labour for low wages, or to make a rapid fortune, or to reap a profit without working himself, he had better stop away. He will do no good in Jamaica. He will do no good anywhere. The free blacks are now doing in Jamaica what Englishmen might have done all along, if a blind and narrow-minded legislation had not discouraged them : they are developing into small proprietors, and, as sure as day follows night, the small resident proprietors will be the future strength and mainstay of the colony. Including coolies, only 5 per cent. of the population are engaged on the cultivation of the sugar-cane.

The revenue for 1886, according to a valuable return just issued from the Colonial Office, was £578,323 (from all sources). £91,026 of this was raised for parochial and municipal purposes and £13,948 for immigration purposes. Over 51 per cent. of the general revenue (£473,348) is raised by duties of customs, more than half being duties on food imported for the use of the population.   Wheaten flour pays 8s. the barrel of 196 lbs. ; meal, 2s. the barrel ; rice, 3s. for every 100 lbs. ; salt meat, 15s. the barrel of 200 lbs. weight ; dried and salted fish, 3s. 4d. the 100 lbs. ; Indian corn, 4d. the bushel, &c. The average value of the yearly exports does not come up to three times the revenue.   The exports for 1887 were valued at £1,280,118 ; of which the United Kingdom took £509,429 ; foreign countries £710,449 ; and the Colonies £60,240.

The imports for the year 1886 were valued at £1,325,603, of which £642,412 were British, £480,341 foreign, and £182,850 from other colonies.

Elementary education is left to private enterprise ; there were 663 schools with 57,557 scholars ; small fees are charged, and they are generally collected.   Grants in aid are given. There are two training colleges for male and female teachers, supported from public funds.   There are a few endowed schools and some scholarships tenable at English universities.   More has been said on this subject in the chapter "Religion and Education."

There is an official Privy Council, or the usual type, for executive purposes.

The Legislative Council is composed of nine elective and six official members, but the Governor can raise the number of the latter to nine.   The Governor presides, and controls the initiation of all money votes.   There is a reserved civil list, in which this body can make no changes.   The present rule is that two-thirds of the elective members decide ordinary financial questions.   The franchise is conferred on the occupier of a dwelling assessed to poor rates combined with payment of 10s. taxes.   Possession of property in respect to which 30s. taxes have been paid.   An annual salary of £50.   There are 9,298 voters.

There is a Mayor and Town Council at Kingston, and there are thirteen other Parochial Boards in the island.   They have nine to fifteen elective members and two official members each. The franchise is the same as for the Legislative Council, and the number of voters is therefore the same for the whole island, distributed.   These bodies have no power of assessing or levying taxes, but they have funds allotted them for parish objects, of which they control the expenditure.   The several direct taxes on land, houses, horses, carriages, etc., are handed over to the parishes in which they have been collected. They are the only direct taxes levied. The land-tax came to about £12,000 in 1886. The total revenues expended by these boards in 1886 were £91,026 1s. 3½d. These boards have jurisdiction over roads, markets, sanitation, poor relief, water-works, and pounds.

The public debt of Jamaica is £1,552,543. There are sixty-four miles of railway, and 664 miles of telegraphs.

The Royal Mail steamers call bi-monthly, and the cargo boats of the same company arrive bi-monthly from Southampton. The West India and Pacific steamers from Liverpool call monthly. There is frequent communication with the United States. Weekly steamers leave Kingston for the outports. The total tonnage entered and cleared in 1886 was 881,516 tons, of which 710,485 tons were British.

The Turks and Caicos Islands are dependencies of Jamaica. There is a Legislative Board, composed of not less than two or more than four nominated members, appointed by the Governor of Jamaica; together with the commissioner and the judge there are not to be over six members. This Board determines matters of taxation and expenditure and other purely local matters, under the initiative of the commissioner, and subject to the approval of the Governor of Jamaica. There are seven elementary schools supported by Government, with an attendance of 800 children. There is one Wesleyan school with eighty-five attendances. There are private schools. Education is compulsory. There is communication with Boston viâ Hayti. These islands were first settled from Bermuda; the population of about 5,000 shows a larger proportion of white blood to African than in most other islands. The revenue for 1886 was £7,505, of which £5,212 was from customs. There are export duties on salt, 10 per cent.; and on cave earth, 2s. per ton. The trade is almost wholly with foreign parts.

Guiana.

It is not at first sight so certain that it would be advisable for this colony to be included in the Caribbean Confederation, as is the case with the other West Indies. It is in itself a territory so vast, that were it to develop in proportion to its extent, it might well stand alone. On the other hand, were

the British West Indian Islands to commence that movement
in advance, which their geographical position and their natural
capacities entitle them to look forward to, the relative position
would not be so different.   Mere extent of territory is not
always a just measure taken by itself alone.   Jamaica and
Trinidad, and the other islands as a whole, could not only
produce immense wealth for export, but may be centres of vast
commercial movements.   The British Islands could well support a population of 5 or 6 millions by agriculture, industries,
commerce, and fisheries.   In course of time the advantages of
confederation would be so apparent — it would bring full
measures of local self-government, the development of local
wealth and general security and public order—that Hayti and
San Domingo would probably be glad to join.   Anyhow, this
British Confederation could be the centre of such a general
commercial and industrial movement, that Guiana would find
many advantages in being a member.

It is three centuries since the Dutch first commenced to
settle in these parts.   After being alternately held by Holland,
France, and England, the present Guiana was ceded to Great
Britain in 1814.   It is unfortunate that the exact boundaries
were not more clearly determined before now, because the
frontier is in dispute, due to its richness in gold.   A question
that might have been settled without any difficulty when the
land was only of hypothetical value, takes very different proportions when masses of gold are supposed to underlie the
surface.   It is to be hoped the whole boundaries will be
definitely, and fairly for all interests, marked or mapped out
before long.   It is quite likely, however, that a closer acquaintance will prove that auriferous deposits of value lie nearer
than the Venezuelan borders.   The advantages of auriferous
deposits that admit of being worked at a profit will be chiefly
in the population that will be attracted by them.   The real
future wealth of Guiana will be due to the development of its
general resources, but which development, without this attrac-
tion to bring population, might have to be long waited for.

British Guiana is now reckoned to have 109,000 square
miles; for a long while it was deemed to be less—about
76,000 square miles—so little interest was taken in the matter.
The estimated population at the close of 1886 was officially
stated at 274,311.   Of this number, 68,759 were East Indian

coolies (17,144 under indenture of service, 35,602 not under indenture, and 16,013 children). There were also 1,266 adult Chinese, and 285 Chinese children. The approximate number of East Indian coolies not resident on estates was 30,516 ; so about 38,200 coolies would be resident on estates under cultivation. The origin of the population of 1886 was officially returned as follows :—Aborigines, 7,426; the East Indies, 94,782 ; China, 3,346 ; Portugal, 11,847 ; Africa, 4,231 ; natives of British Guiana (not being aborigines) and the West Indies generally, 152,679. In 1886 there were 105 sugar estates, comprising 76,203 acres. The 1885 sugar crop was 124,283 hogsheads. There were 5,218 acres of plaintain cultivation. Attention is given in some places to the cultivation of coffee and cacao. The East Indians now grow a good deal of rice at the back of the sugar estates. The colony is notably rich in forest products ; such as india-rubber, ballata, and other gums. Gold is known to be largely disseminated. There were about 2,000 workers at the diggings in 1887.

The total revenue from all sources in 1886 was £495,362, of which about 48 per cent. were from duties of customs. In comparison with Jamaica, the duties on imported food are light. Flour pays $1 the barrel of 196 lbs. ; corn-meal, 25 cents. per 100 lbs. ; and rice, 25 cents. per 100 lbs. The revenue is collected under four heads : General revenue, £446,025 ; Borough of Georgetown revenue, £39,198 ; New Amsterdam revenue, £4,742 ; and village revenue (tax assessed on house and landed property therein), £5,396. There is a public debt of £446,700. The exports were valued in 1887 at £1,842,585, of which Great Britain received £1,071,432 ; foreign countries, £690,099 ; and other colonies, £81,054. The imports for the year 1886 were £1,436,297, of which £787,053 were British ; £365,025 foreign; and £284,219 from other colonies. The total tonnage entered and cleared was 627,845 tons, of which 400,819 tons were British.

The central Administration of Education is invested in an inspector of schools. Local control is conducted by managers, who are usually ministers of religion. In the year 1886 there were 160 schools, with 18,919 scholars. The educational grant was £17,369. There is a first-grade grammar school, and one scholarship tenable at a university in England.

The "constitution" of British Guiana is rather complicated, but its practical result is to give absolute power to the Governor. There is a Court of Policy, five of whose members are officials and five are nominated by an Elective College. The Elective College that nominates the five members is itself composed of only seven members, elected for life by a restricted suffrage. The franchise for electing these electors is conferred for a freehold of three acres under cultivation ; a house worth £20 per annum; occupancy of six acres or house wo th £40 per annum. In the towns : occupancy of house worth £104 3s. 4d., or rented at £25 per annum. Income of £125. Payment of £4 3s. 4d. in direct taxes. There are 1,233 voters in a population of 274,000. The senior nominated member retires every year, and then the seven life members of the Elective College send in two names, and the Court of Policy (where the Governor commands, by his casting vote, an official majority) selects which of these two it pleases. This Court of Policy authorises all expenditure subject to obtaining supplies therefor from another court, called the Combined Court. The introduction of all votes rests with the Governor. He can also veto any measure at any stage of its proceedings. The Combined Court is composed of the above Court of Policy and five "financial" representatives, who are elected for two years by the same electors who elect the seven life members of the College of Electors. These five "financial" members can only deal with financial questions, but they may not discuss any item in the estimates submitted by the Governor with the view of altering it, unless by the Governor's express permission. This Combined Court imposes taxation and votes ways and means ; the civil list is usually enacted for seven years. With the above limitations this Court has the power to control expenditure, limited by usage to striking out or decreasing a vote. The Governor here also can veto any measure at any stage of its proceedings.

Perhaps a more complicated machinery for carrying out the absolute commands of a Governor was never yet invented. It does not work smoothly ; terrible wrangles are reported from time to time, due to the financial representatives insisting upon being heard, and objecting to items. The system is really a survival from the old Dutch rule, and was devised for the purpose of upholding a monopoly of all the cultivation and produce of the colony in favour of a home guild.

There is a Corporation at Georgetown composed of thirteen elective members. The suffrage to elect a member is conferred by occupancy of premises valued at $250. This Corporation has authority to levy and expend town taxes. The amount levied in 1886 was £39,198. There is a Board of Superintendence for New Amsterdam, composed of seven elective members. The suffrage to elect a member is conferred on possessors of any tenement rated at $400. This Board can raise and expend taxes for the town, but must submit its estimates to the Governor and Court of Policy. There are Village Councils possessing three elective members and one nominated member. The suffrage in this case is on holders of one-fourth of a "village lot;" the ownership of lots worth over $500 confers two votes. These Councils can assess rates and expend the sums (within a fixed limit) under the control and approval of the Central Village Board, of which the Governor and Court of Policy is the major part.

There are twenty-one miles of railway and 272 miles of telegraph. The Royal Mail steamers call bi-monthly. The French Cie. Générale Transatlantique and the Dutch line from Holland (touching at Havre), call monthly. A New York line calls every six weeks. There are also many other steamers calling from time to time.

Trinidad.

At the close of the year 1886 the population of Trinidad was 178,270, being a little over 101 to the square mile. This island could easily support, by agriculture and commerce, 1,500,000 inhabitants. The males exceed the females in number by about 15,000. Many able-bodied men come here from the other British West Indies to work for the higher wages procurable, but do not always bring their wives and families. Among the coolies also males preponderate. As regards what may be called the native resident population there will be an excess of females. During the three years 1884-6, 7,038 coolies were landed. In the latter year the sum of £41,276 was expended on immigration, the fixed establishment costing £3,552 more. English is. the official language, but French and Spanish are much spoken. The strong French element is due to the descendants of the numerous refugees from San Domingo and Hayti that fled on the outbreak of the insurrectionary troubles on the island divided between these two black republics. The Spanish and French elements (a good deal of which is aristocratic in origin) have given a *cachet* to this colony possessed by none other under the Crown. They are as enterprising as the British element, and, perhaps from not being bound to the same narrow views about the all-potency of sugar, they have helped to keep up the cultivation of cacao and other valuable productions for which this island is now getting so good a name. Trinidad has much of that about it which gives it a right to be looked on as a kind of metropolis—a splendid tropical climate, land marvellously rich, a magnificent natural harbour, and a grand geographical position for trade.

The acreage of this magnificent colony is 1,123,000 acres, of which only 313,585 acres are in hand, as follows: Sugar-cane, 52,163; cacao and coffee, 43,363; ground provisions, 18,053; cocoa-nuts, 2,767; pasture, 6,242; uncultivated, 190,997.

The revenue for the year 1886, for all purposes (general and municipal), was £474,659, of which 37½ per cent. was raised by duties of customs. In this colony only about 10 per cent. of the revenue is raised in food imports. The yearly exports average in value between five and six times the amount levied by taxation. In 1887 they were valued at £2,509,140; of which the United Kingdom received £949,622, foreign countries £1,504,709, and British Colonies £54,809. Export duties are levied on sugar, molasses, rum, cocoa, and coffee for immigration purposes, and on asphalte and petroleum for general purposes. The imports for the year 1886 totalled £2,503,514, of which £666,499 were British, £1,566,011 foreign, and £271,004 from other colonies. Trinidad does a large trade with Venezuela and with France. A far larger trade might be done with Venezuela to the mutual profit of both, but the illiberal, if no worse, conduct of the latter State hinders this. Venezuela is probably jealous of Trinidad; a puerile and unbusinesslike sentiment.

There are two kinds of schools: secular schools, entirely under Government control; and denominational schools, aided by grants. The former number 53 with 51 masters, 10 assistant masters, 12 mistresses, and 67 assistant and work mistresses, and 70 pupil teachers, paid monitors, and normal students, with 4,212 attendances of scholars. The latter number 64 with 6,315 attendances. Fees usually paid, 3d. weekly; some schools ask 2s. a month; model schools, 5s. a month. Reduced rates are allowed for over one child in a family. Besides the above there are several private adventure schools, including a large convent (R.C.) boarding and day school for girls. There are thirteen estate schools, under the Presbyterian Coolie Mission, with 453 pupils. For higher education there is the Queen's Royal College (secular), and its affiliated Roman Catholic institution, the College of the Immaculate Conception. In the year 1886 the former had 65 students, and the latter 220. Between them they have three scholarships of £150 each, tenable for three years at a university in Great Britain or Ireland. The Government primary schools can send yearly three scholars for three years each to the Queen's Royal College. There is a training college for male teachers, in connection with the boys' model school, for 12 resident and 7 non-resident students. Altogether in Trinidad there are about 13,500 children attending school, or less than 1 in 13 of the population. The school attendances should be nearly double this at least.

A volunteer corps was established in 1879. There is a rifle association of 235 members. The police force is 435 strong.

There is an Executive Council of 3 members, nominated by the Governor, who presides. The Legislative Council consists of 7 officials and 8 nominated members *for life*, selected from the principal merchants and planters. All questions of taxation and expenditure must be initiated by the Executive (the Governor). A committee of the Council, nominated by the Governor, prepares the estimates before they are laid before the Council to be passed. The Government of Trinidad is, therefore, a pure bureaucracy.

There are two municipalities in the island : Port of Spain, with 16 elected members, and San Fernando, with 10. All those occupying a house of an annual value of £40 have votes. These municipalities may levy rates on houses and real property, and on certain licences within their limits, and expend the proceeds. In 1886 Port of Spain levied £16,550, and San Fernando £4,701.

Trinidad has no municipal debt, but there is a Government debt of £559,380.

There are 65 miles of railway, and 63 of telegraph.

Coasting steamers start three times weekly, plying between Port of Spain, San Fernando, and other coast towns. Thirty-five steamers call monthly from all parts, taking mails. The tonnage entered and cleared in 1886 was 1,196,076 tons, of which 774,916 tons were British.

Barbados.

If a people may be judged by what they think of themselves, the Barbadians have little to complain of. As things go in this world, perhaps they have nothing to complain of. But if Barbados is anything, it is British, and where are there Britons without grievances? The grievance of the Barbadians is the joy of London. When sugar is low in price they growl; and now the Conference, other things aiding, has made sugar $\frac{1}{2}$d. lb. dearer in England, and our housewives draw long faces and Barbadians rejoice. It is said the island produced, in 1886, 45,768 hogsheads of sugar, and 33,218 puncheons of molasses. It sometimes ships 10,000 to 12,000 more hogsheads of sugar than this. The island has only 166 square miles. Somebody must make a lot of money. This small area, at the close of the year 1886, held a population of 180,000. The "fair" sex predominated by nearly 18,000, and, as they are reported to work better than the men for half the wages, employers should have a good time of it. The Barbadian black man is a skilled labourer, and he emigrates for good wages by which he may save up money; but he will only leave his island to get higher wages than are usually earned or current in the other West Indies. He earns more because he works more, or does more. The general revenue raised in 1886 was £136,286, of which 60 per cent. was raised by customs duties. But the duties on food stuffs imported for popular use are light compared to some other West Indian colonies. A large customs revenue does not imply heavy duties, but the contrary. Besides the general revenue, there is a parish revenue of about £58,000 a year, and a road commissioner's revenue of about £8,000. The imports for the year 1886 were valued at £863,491, of which £302,763 were British, £360,510 foreign, and £200,218 from other colonies. The exports for 1887 were valued at £739,911, of which £190,240 were sent to the

United Kingdom, £309,500 to foreign countries, and £240,171 to other colonies.

Education in Barbados is placed under the administration of a central board appointed by the Governor. Local control is conducted by the clergy of the districts, assisted by school committees. There are 199 schools with a nominal roll of about 20,000 scholars, the average attendances being 11,530. There is a yearly grant for elementary education which is not to exceed £15,000 a year. There is a college affiliated to Durham University under the administration of the S.P.G. ; it possesses several theological scholarships of the yearly value of £30 each, and four island scholarships of the yearly value of £40 each. There is a grammar school, with an average attendance of 140 pupils. There is another first-grade school with 43 pupils. There are four Barbadian scholarships, endowed by the colony under the direction of the Education Board, worth £175 a year each, tenable for four years at Cambridge or Oxford. There are some other grants in aid to scholars. There is a first-grade girls' school with 86 pupils. There is a juvenile reformatory.

The Legislative Council consists of nine members, two of whom are officials, and seven are unofficial nominees of the Crown, on the recommendation of the Governor for the time being. The assent of this Council is necessary to all Bills. The House of Assembly consists of twenty-four members, all elective. The franchise is conferred as follows :—Freehold of value of £5 ; receipt of rents of annual value of £5 ; occupancy of property assessed to parish rates at £15 ; income of £15 a year; payment of parish taxes, £1 a year (£2 a year in St. Michael's) ; occupancy of lodging of £15 a year ; profession of barrister, solicitor, or doctor ; university degree. This assembly is elected annually. There are 4,200 registered voters, of whom 2,126 voted at last election. Previous to the Franchise Act of 1884, the number of registered electors was only 1,641. The vote is by ballot ; there is a Corrupt Practices Act; there are revising barristers. The House has an elected speaker and other officers, a mace, and so forth. The qualifications for a member of this assembly are as follows :— A freehold of thirty acres of land, and a house on it worth not less than £300; the ownership of real estate not under £1,500; real property rented at £120 a year; or £200 a year from all sources.

The Governor has a negative vote. The Home Government retains the power of withholding or disallowing any Bill.

There is an Executive Committee presided over by the Governor. This committee introduces all money votes, prepares all estimates, and initiates all Government measures. Its present composition is as follows:—The Governor, the Commander of the Troops, the Colonial Secretary, the Attorney-General, one nominated member of the Legislative Council (all of whom are already officials or nominated), and four members of the House of Assembly nominated by the Governor.

There is an Executive Council composed of three officials and one unofficial member, who is nominated by the Governor.

The Barbadian Assembly, under the directions of the executive committee, levies taxation and votes supplies. There is no regular civil list, but the salaries of several officers are secured, more or less permanently, by special Acts. Business proceeds by Bills read three times and by resolutions. Private members can move an address to the Governor in executive committee requesting that certain acts may be done involving expenditure, or requesting certain Bills or resolutions may be presented to the Assembly which will involve expenditure. Private members introduce Bills demanding the granting of powers to local bodies to raise loans.

There are eleven parish vestries, three of which have sixteen elected members, and eight have ten elected members each; each parish has an unofficial nominated member. The franchise is the same as for the Assembly. These vestries have the power to levy rates which are subject to confirmation by the Governor in council. They have charge of the expenditure of the church, poor, and other parish rates. The chief tax is a land tax. The total revenue of the vestries for 1886 was about £58,000.

There are thirty-three road commissioners, all of whom are nominated by the Governor. They are charged with the expenditure on roads only. The revenue is derived from taxes on land and animals, and came to the sum of £8,c60 13s. 2d. in 1886.

There are twenty-three miles of railway, and thirty-five miles of telegraph wires. The West Indian and ' Panama Telegraph Company has a station here. There are bi-monthly mails to and from England which touch at other West Indian islands. There is a weekly steamer to and from Liverpool, and a direct monthly steamer to and from London. The line of steamers to and from Brazil and New York touches bi-monthly. The total tonnage inwards and outwards in 1886 was 916,242 tons, of which 841,791 was British tonnage.

The Bahamas.

The Bahamas Archipelago lies north of Cuba and that island which is divided between the black republics of Hayti and San Domingo. In 1886 the population was estimated to be 47,287. The females are in excess of the males by about 2,200. The number of whites—over 10,000—is large for the British West Indies. Next to Jamaica the area of the Bahamas group is the greatest of the West Indian Island Governments, but how much. of the 2,921 square miles are serviceable for purposes of settlement is unknown; some say one-third is uncultivable. The chief industry just now is the sponge fishery, which occupies about 4,000 men, and realises about £60,000 a year, and pine-apple and other fruit cultivation for the American market. The bulk of the population, while decent in appearance, is but poorly off; and well they may be, for it appears they are made the victims of a far-reaching truck system, than which nothing is more calculated to impede progress and destroy the life out of the homes of the poor. We know the evil the truck system did in Great Britain, and how difficult it was to eradicate it. It would appear there are like powerful influences on foot in the Bahamas to hinder the most necessary reforms in a similar direction. In this place, also, the machinery of public opinion practically does not exist, and the discontent of the people who suffer finds no utterance. The House of Assembly of this colony is, as will be seen, unusually representative for the West Indies. But nothing is better known or more established by daily experience than that such bodies in small communities can be manipulated by powerful and established interests. An assembly that allows the truck system to live does not do its duty. A confederation of all the West Indies would make scandals of this nature difficult, if not impossible, to keep on foot in any place, as they are kept on foot now.

The general revenue for the year 1886 was £43,338, of

which 86 per cent. was raised by duties of customs. The duty on wheat flour is 2s. 6d. per barrel, and 10 per cent. *ad valorem ;* and on corn-meal, 2s. the barrel. There were also crown land and salt fund revenues which brought £542. The average yearly exports are less in value than four times the taxation. The imports for 1886 were valued at £189,410, of which £30,935 were British, £156,383 foreign, and £2,092 from other colonies. The exports in 1887 were valued at £150,390, of which £15,486 were sent to the United Kingdom, £132,702 to foreign countries, and £2,202 to other colonies.

Education is controlled by a central committee nominated by the Governor. Local committees, which are partly elected, exercise local supervision only. There are compulsory clauses which are not always enforced. There are thirty-three unsectarian Government schools with 3,503 scholars, five aided schools with 356 scholars, and 31 Church of England and 15 private schools with 1,800 scholars.

There is an Executive Council composed of the Governor and nine members, and a Legislative Council similarly constituted. They are composed of five officials and four members nominated by the Governor. Their composition may be altered at the Governor's pleasure by increasing the official or the nominative element, but there must be no more than nine of both. There is a House of Assembly of twenty-nine members, all elective. The qualifications for a vote are as follows :—ownership of land of the value of £5, occupancy of a house of the annual value, in new Providence Island of £2 8s., in the other islands £1 4s. There are 5,811 voters. No Bill sent up from the Assembly can become law until it passes the Council. The Assembly levies all taxation and votes all supplies. Money votes and financial proposals are initiated in it, but by the recommendation of the Governor. There is a large civil list reserved, over which the Assembly has no jurisdiction. The Governor can veto any Bill. He can reserve for the Queen's pleasure any Bill which changes the number of officials or their emoluments, or which imposes differential duties.

There are no telegraphs. In the summer there is monthly communication with New York, and in winter fortnightly. Americans in delicate health seek Nassau in New Providence

Island during winter; the climate being very suitable to those constitutions requiring not too dry a heat, and those suffering from nervous diseases. The proximity of the Bahamas to Florida will have an invigorating effect as the latter country develops. The Bahaman labourers will get better wages and money wages; and the truck system, if not done away with by legislative enactment, will be abolished by natural causes.

The total tonnage inwards and outwards in 1886 was 209,996 tons, of which 61,057 tons were British.

This colony has a public debt of £87,896. About the year 1500 all the aborigines inhabiting the Bahama Islands were transferred to Cuba to work the mines. Needless to say they were all destroyed, or, as we should in these days euphemistically say, "They died off."

Honduras.

This dependency has an area of 6,400 square miles, and only 30,000 population. As a colony it has disappointed the expectations formed of it from time to time, and it is likely to continue to do so. People may say what they like against the Central American States, and they deserve a good deal of what is said against them, but for all that pushing men and emigrants will prefer them to this dead-alive place where there is nothing to induce men to settle. Much of the available land is held by large holders who will not sell. The proprietors would seem to hope to get coolies instead of emigrants, or free labourers, on account of their present cheapness as labourers. If the Colonial Office encourages this sentiment, the degradation of this colony will be permanently ensured. If it were to be included in a Confederation with the West Indian Islands, in course of time real colonists and genuine labour might be attracted to the place, and it would then participate in the general onward movement which otherwise it will lie outside of. In these days of competition for men, emigrants will not go to a place except the inducements given are at least equal to those to be had elsewhere. Even free labour will not go to a place except high wages, leaving a margin to save, are procurable; and these labourers will want facilities of purchase of land, to settle on as owners if they deem fit. There are places in Central and South America, at least quite equal to Honduras, where emigrants are offered good land for almost nothing, because their very presence brings wealth, and where good wages are to be had. Coolie labour has its admitted advantages, but it does not make great colonies, and where it is manifestly unsuitable it demoralises the social system by placing labour on a wrong basis. If Honduras gets a free local self government, and becomes a part of a powerful confederacy, it will undoubtedly begin that onward march for which it has been so long waiting.

The revenue in 1886 was $271,806. The dollar of Guatemala is the standard. Its value in 1886 was 3s. 1d.; this makes the revenue £41,903, over 54 per cent. of which were from customs and harbour dues. The exports in 1887 were of the value of £280,047, of which £180,675 were sent to Great Britain, £99,067 to foreign parts, and £305 to neighbouring colonies. The imports in 1886 were valued at £235,953, of which £94,029 were British, £140,421 foreign, and £1,503 from other colonies. There is a public debt of £53,750. The total tonnage entered and cleared was 237,254 tons, of which 100,992 tons were British. There are steamers to New Orleans every ten days; monthly steamers call from New York and Costa Rica; the London and Nassau line calls every five weeks; the West Indian, Colon, and Liverpool line calls monthly.

In 1886 there were 25 schools, with 2,527 pupils on rolls, and 1,770 average attendances, or about 1 in 17 of the population—a very backward condition of things.

The Legislative Council consists of 6 officials and 6 unofficial members, nominated on the Governor's recommendation. The Governor's power in this colony may be considered almost absolute, as he commands in the Council an official vote which can carry any question. It is hardly reasonable to expect such a place to be deemed a "colony" by emigrants. Under such conditions no place can ever really thrive.

Grenada and the Windward Islands Confederacy.

The only apparent object in forming this Confederacy (if it may so be called) of the Windward Islands, is to have a Governor in common, and a common Court of Appeal composed of the chief justices of the several islands. Barbados was until recently included in this "Confederacy," but it found it expedient to leave it. By the Letters Patent of 17th March,

1885, each island retains its own institutions, and is presided over by a resident administrator who also does the functions of Colonial Secretary. The several islands have neither legislation, nor laws, nor revenue, nor tariffs in common. This group is composed of Grenada (with part of the Grenadines), St. Vincent (with the remainder of the Grenadines), St. Lucia, and Tobago.

St. Lucia, St. Vincent, and Tobago have concurrent (religious) endowment of £1,500, £2,525, and £1,000 per annum respectively.

In 1886 the population of Grenada was 47,364, or 356 to the square mile. There was an excess of females compared to males to the number of about 2,300. This island possesses all the necessary elements to ensure success. It is getting remarked for the cocoa it produces. It has had to struggle against much adverse circumstances. Its present position leaves much to be desired, but the mere fact of its being no worse off is a proof of latent strength and energy which should encourage its well-wishers. The number of peasant owners has largely increased in recent years. There is room for the planter and the great or small capitalist who is not afraid to pay a fair day's wages for a fair day's work.

The imports into Grenada were valued in 1886 at £120,338, of which £53,553 were British, £17,741 foreign, and £49,053 from other colonies. The exports for 1887 were £180,691, of which £159,805 were sent to the United Kingdom, £9,946 to foreign countries, and £10,940 to other colonies.

The revenue from all sources in 1886 was £45,286, of which 47½ per cent. was levied by duties of customs. The revenue is collected under five headings : for general purposes, £42,234 ; for immigration purposes, £1,407 ; St. George's town receipts, £1,190 ; Grenville harbour receipts, £306, and village revenue, £148.

The schools are separately under the management of the ministers of the different religious sects who are under the supervision of a central administration—a board appointed by the Governor—half the members being Roman Catholic. The average attendance at the 2 elementary Government schools and the 23 aided schools in 1886 was 1,570 pupils. Fees are charged. Attendance is not compulsory. Building and annual grants depend on results of inspection. There is also a grammar school partly supported by public funds. The Legislative Council is composed of 6 officials and the Governor (who presides), and 7 unofficial members, who are nominees of the Governors.

The language of Grenada is a French patois for the population generally, but English is the official language.

There are parochial boaids, half the members of which are elected, and half nominated by the Governor. The electors are those who occupy premises rented at £20 a year, or who pay 10s. a year rates or taxes. They can levy rates up to a limit fixed by law, as well as certain dues; they can expend the sums so raised, subject to supervision by the central Government.

The Governor's power in Grenada is absolute. He commands an official majority in all the councils. The only chance for any redress of a grievance or a wrong is the doubtful issue of a petition to Downing Street. No European colonists are likely to settle in a colony so circumstanced. The steamers of the Royal Mail Steam Packet Company call bi-monthly. The total tonnage inwards and outwards in 1886 was 298,338 tons, nearly all of which was British.

St. Lucia.

At the close of the year 1886 the population of St. Lucia was 41,791, or nearly 176 to the square mile. The females in excess of males in this island were only about 650. There are about 2,400 East Indians. This colony was finally taken possession of by England 85 years ago. For the previous 170 years of its history it was alternately in French and British occupation. For the first few years the Caribs succeeded in killing and expelling all European colonists, but eventually they had to succumb, and were finally destroyed in this island as elsewhere. Only about one-fifth of this island is cultivated; how much of it is unsuitable for cultivation is unknown, and any estimate would be unreliable. That a great field for enterprise exists here under remarkably favourable circumstances is a fact not admitting of doubt. A splendid soil and climate that will grow anything; a grand position for trade and the disposal of produce; good labour for those who are willing to pay for it; magnificent scenery, and a healthy climate for the tropics; a genially disposed people. A young Englishman, with capital and some enterprise, who desires to carve out a future for himself, would do as well, if not better here, as in the distant East. There are now over 14,000 freeholders in this colony. There is a central "usine" on the principle established at Martinique, in which the (local) Colonial Government has an interest.

St. Lucia has been chosen for a chief coaling station, and Castries Harbour is being strongly fortified and garrisoned.

The laws partake of the French systems. A code framed on the ancient laws of the island was drawn up and became law in 1879.

The revenue for 1886 was £44,704 from all sources; 47½ per cent. of which was from customs duties and wharfages. There is an export duty of 4d. on every 100 lb. of sugar. This island levies a higher excise duty on rum and other spirits than is usually the case in the other West Indies; in 1886 it came to £11,122. The revenue is divided into ordinary revenue, £38,009; for immigration purposes, £3,722; Crown lands revenue, £207; Castries town revenue, £2,018; village house tax, £745.

Education is backward; only about 1 in 15 of the population receive instruction.

There is an Executive Council of the usual type. The Legislative Council is composed of 5 officials, and 5 unofficial members nominated by the Governor's recommendation. The same as in Grenada, the Governor in this island is absolute. The Administrator and Colonial Secretary of the island presides at the Council.

The imports were valued in 1886 at £122,284, of which £63,624 were British, £43,971 foreign, and £14,671 from other colonies. The exports for 1887 were £105,207, of which £28,980 were sent to the United Kingdom, £58,565 to foreign countries, and £17,662 to other colonies. The total tonnage cleared inwards and outwards was 435,425 tons, of which 392,640 tons were British. The British mail steamers call bi-monthly, and there is other steam communication.

There is a Town Board for Castries, consisting of 3 to 5 members, nominated by the Governor. It is responsible for the funds appropriated for town purposes by the central Government.

The language spoken is a French patois.

St. Vincent.

The population of this island in December, 1886, was 42,000, or 320 to the square mile. The females were about 2,200 in excess of the males. There were 192 so-called Caribs still on this island, but few if any are of pure race ; they are noted for their intrepidity in shipping cargo through breakers. There is a Carib reserve. There are about 2,000 East Indian coolies, imported by the sugar planters. The Caribs of this island joined the French flag in the great wars between England and France. After Sir Ralph Abercrombie took possession of it by force of arms, Caribs to the number of 5,080 were transported, in March, 1797, to the Island of Rattan in the Bay of Honduras, where they died of scurvy.

There are between thirty and forty churches and chapels in this island belonging to the Church of England and the Wesleyans, three or four are Roman Catholic, and one is Presbyterian. Education is rather backward ; only one in ten of the population attending schools.

The revenue from all sources in 1886 was £30,877, nearly 60 per cent. of which was raised by import and export duties and harbour dues. Flour pays 4s. a barrel ; meal, 2s. a barrel; beef and pork, 12s. 6d. on 200 lbs. ; rice, ½d. per lb., &c. The imports for the same year were valued at £91,185, of which £47,214 were British, £8,496 foreign, and £35,475 from other colonies. The exports for 1887 were £70,746, of which £21,789 were sent to the United Kingdom, £40,153 to foreign countries, and £8,534 to other colonies. The tonnage inwards and outwards was 346,650 tons, of which 339,363 tons were British. The mail steamer calls bimonthly.

The revenue is collected under four heads: the general revenue, £27,467 ; revenue for immigration purposes, £1,705 ; Kingstown revenue, £1,473 ; and village revenue, consisting of a rate on houses in the towns, £230.

There is a Legislative Council, consisting of four officials and four nominees of the Governor, presided over by the

Administrator and Colonial Secretary. The Governor of the Windward Islands is absolute in this island.

St. Vincent is remarkable for being (with Martinique) the home of the dreaded lance-headed snake. Hot springs of undoubted medicinal value exist in the hills.

Tobago.

In 1886 the population of Tobago was only 18,000, being about 158 to the square mile. There are about 650 more females than males. This is a very fine island, and only one-seventh of it is cultivated. Its proximity to Trinidad—less than twenty miles distant—is worth considering by people who are on the look-out for a place where good land may be had cheap. The island has not been fortunate. It suffered greatly from much of its cultivated lands being in the hands of the monopolists—absentee merchants and others—who would grow nothing but sugar, and who have now transferred their capital to other places where this cultivation pays better. The *métairie* system is in use. Coolies are asked for by planters, who are willing to pay a part of the cost of their introduction, the public taxes defraying the balance. The system of resident owners of small and moderate-sized holdings, cultivating and personally superintending the cultivation of their property, is what is wanted in this island, and it will doubtless hereafter spread to it. This and other islands offer a really good field for the enterprise of young Englishmen. A good deal of this island is almost unexplored. Education is backward. The mail steamers call once a month. The revenue for 1886 was £8,813, of which 45 per cent. was levied by customs. The imports for the same year were valued at £20,499, of which £11,656 were British, and £8,827 from other colonies. The exports for 1887 were valued at £18,891, of which £8,553 were sent to the United Kingdom, £547 to foreign countries, and £9,791 to other colonies. The tonnage inwards and outwards was 87,049 tons, all of which, except 1,000 tons, was British. There is a Legislative Council of three officials and three nominees of the Governor. The Administrator and Colonial Secretary presides. The Governor of the Windward Islands is absolute in this island.

Antigua and the Leeward Islands Confederacy.

The population of Antigua is said to be stationary now. It has decreased steadily in recent years. It has a population of about 35,000, or 324 to the square mile. The females exceed the males by about 2,400. The revenue in 1886 was £41,323. Sixty-nine per cent. of this was raised by duties of customs, half of which were levied on articles of food imported for the use of the population. This island levies export duties. The total exports average in value from three to four times the taxes levied. In 1887 the exports of Antigua and Barbuda were £159,658, of which £20,910 were sent to the United Kingdom, £115,285 to foreign countries, and £23,490 to other colonies. In 1886 the imports totalled £131,626, of which £63,627 represented British imports, £49,711 foreign imports, and £18,288 imports from other colonies. The tonnage entered and cleared in 1886 came to 380,641 tons, of which 364,991 tons were British.

Antigua is the headquarters of the Leeward Islands Confederacy. This Confederacy has been so brought about and so manipulated and managed that it has thrown discredit upon the time-honoured name of Confederation throughout the whole West Indies. It is a Government powerless in itself to do any good, but which has developed great capacities for hindering any good being done by the several parts. The various islands now comprising this Confederacy are Antigua (with Barbuda), St. Kitts-Nevis (with Anguilla), Montserrat, the Virgin Islands, and Dominica. All these islands had more or less partially popularly elected Assemblies prior to the creation of this Confederacy, but all of them, with the exception of Antigua and Dominica, were over-persuaded, and abrogated their rights in the belief that a full equivalent would be forthcoming in some other way. The whole scheme ended in a concentration of bureaucratic despotism. The islands lost their little local governments and got nothing in return, except a special tax to keep on foot a useless Governor, a staff of officials to help him, and a Legislature powerless for good.

The Leeward Islands Legislative Council is composed of ten nominated members and ten elected members. The nominated members comprise six officials and four unofficial members, the latter being selected from among the elected or unofficial nominated members, as the case may be, of the several Island Councils. The ten elected members are elected from among their own body by the elected or unofficial members of certain Island Councils as follows: The elected members of the Legislative Council of Antigua elect four of their own body, the elected members of the Dominican Assembly elect two of their own body, and the unofficial members of the St. Kitts-Nevis Council elect four of their own body. The President of this Leeward Islands Council is nominated by the Governor from among the members of the Island Councils. The Council itself elects a Vice-President.

The above Council has concurrent legislative powers with the local island legislatures in pretty well everything, and can repeal and alter any act of any local legislature, and no local legislature can do anything not deemed to be in harmony with previous acts of this Council. It can levy no taxation; but passes estimates of the expenditure necessary for federal purposes. And this has to be provided, and voted as a matter of course, by the local (official) councils.

The Council meets once a year, and lasts three years. But the Governor may call it, prorogue it, and dissolve it, when he pleases, and it meets where he selects it shall meet by proclamation.

There are Anglican, Wesleyan, Moravian, and Roman Catholic schools in the Leeward Islands Confederacy, all of which receive grants in aid. School fees are charged, but no child applying is refused. There are 120 aided schools, with an average of 9,000 attendances in the five Governments. A grammar school receives a Government grant of £200 a year at Antigua, and another at St. Kitts has a similar grant.

Antigua has Councils of its own. There is an Executive Council, appointed by the Crown, over which the Governor presides. The Legislative Council is composed of twenty-four members, of whom six are officials, six are nominated by the Governors, and twelve are elected members. The qualification for an elector in a town is the possession of land in fee simple or as a tenant, for not less than six months before the election; in the former case, of the annual value of £13 16s. 8d.; in the latter case, £26 13s. 4d. For a country elector a man must possess ten acres of land in fee simple, or five acres with buildings thereon, or land of value of £111, or one acre of land

and buildings value £222, or a tenancy of not under £88 a year.

There are eleven electoral divisions. The City of St. John has 130 voters; the remaining ten divisions have seventy-eight voters between them. The Council lasts for five years. It has a President and a Vice-President, both nominated by the Governor, and they have casting votes. The Governor controls, besides, the initiation of all money votes. We have here a very fair sample of a dummy Council; it is both packed and overruled by official votes. The electors trouble themselves but slightly about the sham; a councillor gets elected by a couple or three votes sometimes.

There is mail communication bi-monthly with Antigua, the other West Indies, and England, by the Royal Mail Steamship Company, and occasionally by the Scrutton Line of steamers and others. The Quebec and Gulf Ports Line, to and from the United States, also touch.

Antigua has a yeomanry cavalry corps of forty-eight officers and men, and a small artillery force.

The Island of Barbuda is attached to the Presidency of Antigua.

The people of Antigua speak English.

St. Kitts-Nevis.

These two islands had separate governments until recently, when they were united under a single local administration. By their geographical configuration, and their juxtaposition, a single natural harbour is formed, upon either side of which lie the chief towns (Basseterre and Charlestown) of the two islands, in sight and within a few miles of each other. The population of the two islands in December, 1886, was estimated to be about 47,000, or 300 to the square mile, the females being in excess of males by about 2,500. As regards these islands this is due to the emigration of the men to Panama, Trinidad, and the Orinoco mines. The people speak English. The revenue for 1886 was £46,344. About 50 per cent. of this was raised by duties of customs, half of which were levied on articles of food in popular use. St. Kitts is a remarkably well-cultivated island, the soil admitting the use of ploughs. Nevis has to be cultivated by the hoe, being very stony and rocky. There is plenty of water in the latter island, but as it does not flow on the immediate surface it is not utilised, because it is not visible to the eye. There are valuable medicinal springs. The chief, almost the only, cultivation of these islands for export is sugar. The total exports average in value between four and five times the revenue collected. The imports for 1886 were valued at £170,735, of which £73,587 represented British imports, and £78,555 foreign imports, and £18,593 imports from other colonies. The exports for 1887 were valued at £159,971, of which £17,197 were sent to the United Kingdom, £129,817 to foreign countries, and £12,957 to other colonies.

There is an Executive Council composed of such persons as Her Majesty may from time to time appoint. The Legislative Council is made up of 10 officials and 10 members nominated by Government. Of these 7 are to be residents of St. Kitts, and 3 of Nevis. The President of the Islands Government has a deliberative and a casting vote. The Governor, or a nominee he selects, presides. It will be seen that the inhabitants are practically unrepresented, even indirectly; but even if they were represented in any way, this Council has no power. The Council of the Confederacy deals with all local matters for each island. No Council of any kind in a West Indian Government has many other matters to deal with unless they be local matters. In the Leeward Islands Confederate Council the people are all equally unrepresented. The Administration is a pure bureaucracy. The Councils of St. Kitts-Nevis for all practical purposes are mere dummies.

St. Kitts has a horse artillery of 26 men, and 2 troops of cavalry numbering 56 officers and men.

The Island of Anguilla is attached to the St. Kitts-Nevis Presidency. It levies export duties on sugar, rum, molasses, potatoes, arrowroot, and cotton, but it produces little.

The tonnage entered and cleared from St. Kitts-Nevis in 1886 was 380,375 tons, of which 369,983 tons were British.

Royal Mail steamers call bi-monthly, the Scrutton and other lines call at intervals, and there is steam communication with the United States.

The number of ruins in Nevis strikes a new-comer forcibly. The whole island is dotted with them. Nelson was married here, his best man being the Duke of Clarence, afterwards William IV.

Dominica.

The population of Dominica was estimated in December 1886, to be 28,500, or about 98 to the square mile. The females exceed the males by about 2,500. Black women do as much labour as men, but they get 50 per cent. less wages, sometimes only half as much. The island is poor, and the produce cultivated for export is little. The cultivation of the sugar-cane is unsuited to the place. There is a magnificent field for enterprise in this island if only the right men could be got to go there; men who would take a common-sense view of the position, and disregard all routine and precedents. Dominica is incontestably one of the finest of the West Indian islands; but it has never been anything because no other cultivation but that of sugar-cane would be seriously undertaken in the West Indies, except at Trinidad. The heavy rainfall makes the maintenance of roads difficult. Practically speaking there are none, except near the town. For the cultivation of oranges, coffee, limes, and many descriptions of fruit, this island is as good as any place.

The revenue for 1886 was £15,238, about half being raised by duties of customs. The exports average in value about four times the revenue raised. In 1887 the exports were valued at £51,530, of which £15,799 were sent to the United Kingdom, £33,203 to foreign countries, and £2,528 to other colonies. The imports in 1886 were valued at £49,733, of which £20,869 were British, £17,348 foreign, and £11,516 colonial. The tonnage entered and cleared in 1886 was 304,423 tons, of which 302,063 were British.

Why Dominica was selected to be one of the islands of the Leeward Confederacy is not obvious.

It has nothing in common with Antigua, or St. Kitts-Nevis, or the others. The religion of the people is chiefly Roman Catholic. The language is a French patois. It would gain by being included in a Confederation of all the British West Indies.

The island is remarkable and interesting from the wonderful natural phenomena found within so small a compass. The streams of hot water and mineral springs should be of great use to invalids and others when made more accessible.

There is an Executive Council of 7 nominated members and the President of the island.

The Legislative Assembly consists of 2 nominated members, 5 officials, and 7 elected members. The President has a casting vote in the House, and a deliberative and a casting vote in Committee. Before 1865 the Assembly had 19 elected members, and 9 nominated members. The qualifications for an elector are as follows : he must have freehold land or houses of a £4 yearly value, or occupy premises on a tenancy worth £8 a year, or have an income of £25 a year, or pay 15s. a year direct taxes. The qualifications of an electorate matters little when an Assembly can be outvoted by the officials. This is another instance of a dummy Assembly or Council. The Administration is a pure bureaucratic despotism —and worse—for the officials can get rid of responsibility through the Assembly which they control. What would English people say if they saw a thing of this kind in some foreign country ? That the local needs of the island are neglected is only what must be expected.

There are the usual heavy import duties on food ; there are export duties levied on sugar, syrup, molasses, rum, lime-juice, coffee, cocoa, arrowroot, manioc, flour, essences, and horned cattle.

There is a Carib reservation in Dominica, and there are said to be 170 of these people who are nearly, or have a good deal, of the pure breed.

Mr. Froude, speaking of Dominica, page 131, says Labat discovered from the language of the Caribs that they were North American Indians. They called themselves *Benari*, which meant "come from over sea." Their dialect was almost identical with what he had heard spoken of in Florida. If by this is meant the Caribs of the Lesser Antilles—of which Dominica is one—it is not likely to have been the case. When the West Indian Islands were discovered, the Caribs who had possession of the Lesser Antilles had only commenced making warlike raids on the sea coasts of the Greater Antilles. These Caribs also were found located along the mainland coast, from the Amazon northwards, and over the islands as far as the Virgin Islands, but not further north or west. Humboldt said the term " Carib " was derived from the South American Caribs. These Caribs of the Lesser Antilles had only recently taken possession of the islands. They destroyed their predecessors—supposed to be Arowaks. The aborigines of the

Greater Antilles were supposed by many to differ from the Caribs of the Lesser Antilles; they were evidently less warlike. The warlike excursions of the Caribs of the Lesser Antilles were, amongst other things, for the purpose of capturing wives. The points of race are not now to be determined except by such internal evidence as may be sifted from contemporary records. The aborigines have all disappeared from the Greater Antilles. The pure Caribs of the Lesser Antilles are almost, perhaps even quite, extinct. The few people of that name now found at Dominica and St. Vincent are mostly, if not all, "black" Caribs—a cross between the Carib and the African. The pure Caribs, from all accounts, had an appearance curiously suggestive of a Chinese or kindred Eastern origin. These Caribs were evidently a fine race, but untamable—at least they were untamable in those days when the alternative lay between remaining untamable and becoming slaves. The so-called Caribs of the Greater Antilles were made slaves of and died in bondage, leaving no successors. The true Caribs of the Lesser Antilles preferred to die fighting. Who is there now that will not admit that, on the whole, it would have been better had they been permitted to live?

Montserrat.

In the year 1886 the population of Montserrat was 10,500, or 223 to the square mile. The females are in excess of males by about 800. The revenue for 1886 (about half raised by duties of customs) was £5,022, but the expenditure was £645 more. The average exports are valued at about five times the yearly revenue. In 1887 they were valued at £20,944, of which £8,385 were sent to the United Kingdom, £11,809 to foreign countries, and £750 to other colonies. The imports for 1886 totalled £21,087, of which £7,416 were British, £2,792 foreign, and £10,879 from other colonies. The island is noted for its cultivation of limes and its lime-juice; over 1,000 acres of lime trees are owned by the Montserrat Company, Limited. This island has only a nominated Council of 2 officials and 3 unofficial members, presided over by the President of the island, who has a deliberative and a casting vote. Whatever the Governor orders has to be done.

The mail steamers call. The tonnage entered and cleared in 1886 was 325,089 tons, of which 323,058 were British.

The Virgin Islands.

This group in 1886 had only about 5,000 population, or 86 to the square mile. It decreases yearly. It has decreased by 1,500 in the last six years. The blacks are noted for their splendid physique and appearance. They are hardy seamen, intelligent traders. They trade exclusively with the well-known island of St. Thomas, where the Royal Mail steamers call bi-monthly, and others frequently. The revenue for 1886 was £1,447, but is sometimes less, some of which is collected by import duties, and some by export duties. The latter has helped much to ruin these islands. They are levied on cattle, pigs, sheep, goats, salt, charcoal, firewood, sugar-cane, cotton, coffee, sweet potatoes, yams, butter—in fact, on everything cultivated, manufactured, or collected, for export.

There is a nominated Executive Council and a Legislative Council of 3 to 4 officials (when there *are* 3 officials on the islands), and 3 to 4 nominated members. The President (or the official acting as such) has a deliberative and a casting vote. The imports—about £2,500 a year—are from St. Thomas. The tonnage entered and cleared in 1886 was 10,764 tons, of which 9,843 were British.